BEYOND TH

Creswell Crags and its place in a wider European context

MATTHEW BERESFORD

Archaeopress

Archaeopress

Gordon House
276 Banbury Road
Oxford OX2 7ED

www.archaeopress.com

ISBN 978 1 905739 50 9

© Archaeopress and Matthew Beresford
2012

All rights reserved. No part of this book may be reproduced, stored in retrieval system,
or transmitted, in any form or by any means, electronic, mechanical, photocopying or otherwise,
without the prior written permission of the copyright owners.

Printed and bound in Great Britain by
Marston Book Services Ltd, Oxfordshire

Cover image
Ice Age Bison Wall Art by Alisdair McNeal

In memory of Roger Jacobi 1947-2009

Beyond the Ice

Creswell Crags and its place in a wider European context

List of Illustrations ii

Acknowledgements v

Introduction 1

Chapter One: Antiquarian interest & early fieldwork 9

Chapter Two: Armstrong's research and interpretations 22

Chapter Three: Discovery of the rock art at Church Hole Cave, Creswell Crags and its wider implications 36

Chapter Four: Challenging the Creswellian: The way forward 50

Chapter Five: The development of Creswell as a heritage site: a 21st century perspective 63

Chapter Six: Neanderthals and Moderns: the search for Creswell Man 78

Chapter Seven: Final Remarks 93

Chapter Eight: Conclusion 101

Appendix 104

Bibliography 105

LIST OF ILLUSTRATIONS

I.1 – *Location of Creswell Crags* (M. Beresford)
I.2 – *George Stubbs' 'Two Gentlemen Going a shooting, with a view of Creswell Crags, Taken on the Spot', c. 1767, oil on canvas* (Public Domain)
I.3 – *Timber support beam from the medieval wooden mill at Creswell Crags* (M. Beresford)
I.4 – *William Buckland (1784-1856)* (Public Domain)
I.5 – *Leg bones gnawed by hyaenas, with similarities labelled, (left) Buckland's experimental bone, (right) bone of bison from Kirkdale* (Public Domain)
I.6 – *Aerial view of Creswell Crags* (© Creswell Heritage Trust)

1.1 – *The Reverend J Magens Mello (1836-1914* (Public Domain)
1.2 – *Sir William Boyd Dawkins (1837-1929)* (Public Domain)
1.3 – *Robin Hood's Cave during the 19th century excavations* (© Creswell Heritage Trust)
1.4 – *Artefacts from the 19th century excavations at Creswell* (© Creswell Heritage Trust)
1.5 – *The horse engraving from Robin Hood's Cave* (© Creswell Heritage Trust)
1.6 – *Pleistocene fauna of Robin Hood's Cave* (M. Beresford. Source: Boyd Dawkins, 1876)
1.7 – *Upper canine of Machairodus from Robin Hood's Cave* (Boyd Dawkins, 1877)
1.8 – *Bone needle from Church Hole* (Boyd Dawkins, 1877)
1.9 – *Bone awl from Church Hole* (Boyd Dawkins, 1877)
1.10 – *Notched bone from Church Hole cave* (Boyd Dawkins, 1877)
1.11 – *Pleistocene fauna of Church Hole Cave* (M. Beresford, Source: Boyd Dawkins, 1876)

2.1 – *Alan Leslie Armstrong* (© Creswell Heritage Trust)
2.2 – *Excavations at the Pin Hole cave during the 1920s* (© Creswell Heritage Trust)
2.3 – *Bone 'marrow scoop' from Mother Grundy's Parlour* (M. Beresford, redrawn from Armstrong, 1924)
2.4 – *Bone 'engravings' from Mother Grundy's Parlour. Bison (left), Reindeer (middle), Rhinocerous (right)* (M. Beresford, redrawn from Armstrong, 1924)
2.5 – *Possible skinning tool from Mother Grundy's Parlour* (M. Beresford, redrawn from Armstrong, 1924)

2.6 – *Bone reindeer point from Church Hole cave* (Garrod, 1926)
2.7 – *Replica of an engraved bone object of Magdalenian design from Creswell Crags* M. Beresford)
2.8 – *The anthropomorphic engraving from the Pin Hole cave* (Armstrong, 1929)
2.9 – *Typical section of the Pin Hole Cave* (Armstrong, 1937)

3.1 – *Plan of Church Hole cave depicting the twelve 'panels' of Ice Age art* (M. Beresford)
3.2 – *Deer Stag engraving (panel III), showing modern grafitti and 'goatee beard'* (M. Beresford)
3.3 – *Panel VII at Church Hole: are they birds or stylised females?* M. (Beresford)
3.4 – *U-series results from Church Hole and Robin Hood's Cave* (M. Beresford. Source: Pike et al, 2007)
3.5 – *Radiocarbon determinations from human-modified bone and antler from Creswell* (M. Beresford. Source: Pike et al, 2007)
3.6 – *Church Hole Panel VII depicting, in the author's opinion, stylised female forms* (M. Beresford, redrawn from Pettitt 2007)
3.7 – *The Venus Impudique from the Dordogne* (Public Domain)
3.8 – *Gönnersdorf Plaquette 2, with detail of engraving 2b – Note the 'truncating' line at the bottom of the legs* (M. Beresford, redrawn from Pettitt, 2007)
3.9 – *Engraving of a stylised female form on a lamp from the site of Grotte de Courbay* (M. Beresford, redrawn from Pettitt, 2007)
3.10 – *The sorcerer from Les Trois Freres* (Public Domain)

4.1 – *Distribution map reflecting Late Upper Palaeolithic sites contemporary with the Creswellian occupation at Creswell Crags* (after Jacobi & Pettitt, 2009)
4.2 – *Flint tools from Newton Linford: piercer (a), obliquely truncated blade with burin scar (b), retouched blade with en éperon preparation (c), Cheddar point (d)* (M. Beresford, redrawn from Cooper, 2002)
4.3 – *Tanged point from Röke, Sweden* (M. Beresford, redrawn from Larsson, 1991)
4.4 – *Flint tool types from the open site at Mill Farm, Whaley* (M. Beresford. Source: Hart, 1984)
4.5 – *The arctic hare was integral to the lifestyle of Creswell Man* (© Robert Nicholls, www.paleocreations.com)
4.6 – *Engraving the bone point with incised lines helped to hold the projectile in place when hafted* (© Creswell Heritage Trust)
4.7 – *The hafted weapon* (© Creswell Heritage Trust)

5.1 – *The merels boards from Church Hole cave* (M. Beresford)
5.2 – *The cave at Langwith Bassett, where Armstrong discovered Palaeolithic remains in the 1930s* (M. Beresford)
5.3 – *1980s publicity leaflet showing early interpretations of how 'Creswell Man' may have looked* (© Creswell Heritage Trust)
5.4 – *Exhibition space inside the new visitor centre* (© Creswell Heritage Trust)
5.5 – *Visitor figures for Creswell Crags, based on adult visitors undertaking guided cave tours* (M. Beresford. Source: Creswell Heritage Trust)
5.6 – *Skull of the Cheddar Man. Cut marks on the skull are clearly visible to the left of the suture* (© Natural History Museum)
5.7 – *Fossilised lynx phalanges from Pin Hole* (M. Beresford, redrawn from Brothwell, 1981)
5.8 – *Skull fragments found at Robin Hood's Cave in 1969, layer OB and E* (M. Beresford, redrawn from Campbell, 1977)

5.9 – *Table showing human remains from the Creswell caves* (M. Beresford)
5.10 – *Radiocarbon dates from Human remains in the Creswell Heritage Area* (M. Beresford. Source: Chamberlain, 2007)

6.1 – *Skull comparison of a Neanderthal (La Chapelle) and Homo sapiens (Combe Capelle)* (Arthur Keith, 1915)
6.2 – *Châtelperronian blades from the type-site of Grotte des Fées* (M. Beresford, redrawn from Gravina et al. 2005)
6.3 – *Child burial from Laghar Vello, Portugal* (© Guida Casella)
6.4 – *The Lowenmensch carving from Schlestwig-Holstein* (Public Domain)
6.5 – *A bâton-de-commandement found at Gough's Cave, Cheddar Gorge* (M. Beresford, redrawn from Wymer, 1984)
6.6 – *Inuit arrow straightener* (Boyd Dawkins, 1874)
6.7 – *End scraper / burin from Langwith Bassett Cave* (© Creswell Heritage Trust)
6.8 – *Cheddar point from Langwith Bassett Cave* (© Creswell Heritage Trust)

7.1 – *Map of Doggerland showing land mass before sea levels rose* (© David Astbury. Rivers after Coles and Rouillard)
7.2 – *Penknife points from the Final Palaeolithic site at Rookery Farm* (M. Beresford, redrawn from Conneller, 2009)
7.3 – *The Abbots Bromley Horn Dancers, circa. 1915, wearing antler headdresses similar to those found at Star Carr. Were they for ritual, hunting or a ceremonial dance?* (Public Domain)
7.4 – *Prehistoric toolmaker John Lord making replica Ice Age tools during an event at Creswell Crags* (© Creswell Heritage Trust)

Acknowledgements

I have wanted to write about the site of Creswell Crags for quite some time, but I was not sure of which angle to take. It was after a brilliant lecture on the history of Creswell Crags back in the summer of 2008 that I mentioned my wish to the late Roger Jacobi of the Natural History Museum of London, who was quite encouraging in his response. He suggested that I may wish to attempt to collate all the information that was out there and offer up a new interpretative history of the Crags. And so the seed was planted in my head and the foundations laid for what I wanted to look at. So, here, I wish to offer my thanks to Roger who, sadly, passed away before this work was finished.

I have been aided by many other people along the way, particularly my old mentors at the University of Nottingham, Dr. David Marcombe (who sadly had to retire through ill health before this work was completed) and Dr. Sarah Speight, who was once again instrumental in shaping my work from an early stage, as she did for my previous book. I also wish to offer my sincere thanks to the publishing team at Archaeopress, particularly David Davison for his belief and support, and to the many people who gave me permission to use their images.

This work, in its finished form, would have been almost impossible to complete without the richness of the Creswell Research Library archive, and I am indebted to Ian Wall and his team at Creswell for allowing me access to this and pointing me in the right direction from time to time. I particularly wish to thank John Scott, Anna Griffiths, Maria Smith and Rebecca Clay who all, at one time or another, offered advice and judgement on various aspects of the history of Creswell Crags. Also, the staff at the various archives who have helped me along the way, including The National Archives, the Nottinghamshire Archive Office, the Derbyshire Record Office, the Derby Museum, Sheffield Museum, the Natural History Museum and the British Museum, particularly Jill Cook for her expert advice on the mobile art from Creswell.

I must now go back in time and thank the many people who have worked at Creswell Crags over the last one hundred and thirty-four years, without whose work I would have had nothing to debate! These are the Rev. John Magens Mello, Sir William Boyd Dawkins, Thomas Heath, Dr. Robert Laing, Alan Leslie Armstrong, Dr. Charles McBurney, Jeffrey Radley, John Campbell, Simon Collcutt, Rogan Jenkinson, Dr. Roger Jacobi, Dr. Paul Pettitt and Dr. Andrew Chamberlain.

Finally, I must thank the people who were the most crucial to this work, the very people who left behind the evidence that this entire work is based upon: the Ice Age inhabitants of the Creswell caves.

I remember reading Francis Pryor's excellent book *Britain BC* and marvelling how he handled the obligatory 'errors and omissions' part, so here I shall echo his words – 'it is customary to end the acknowledgements part with a formulaic statement to the effect that the errors, biases and omissions owe nothing to the various people mentioned, and are entirely the author's responsibility'. And just like Francis, I really *do* mean it also.

Matthew Beresford
Southwell
Nottinghamshire
September 2010

Introduction

'The Creswell Crags, on the Nottinghamshire-Derbyshire border near Worksop, come as a surprise when one is travelling through this fairly featureless landscape. Suddenly there is an idyllic little valley with a small stream between cliffs of Magnesian Limestone. And in the cliffs are a whole series of small caves, most of which were inhabited at times during the last Ice Age'.

Paul Bahn, *Current Archaeology,* May / June, 2005

In 1769, 10,000 years after the last Ice Age, the prehistoric history of Creswell Crags lay long forgotten. In the gorge that day was an artist by the name of George Stubbs, who stood painting his picture *Two Gentlemen Going a shooting, with a view of Creswell Crags, Taken on the Spot* which shows a medieval wooden water mill in the background. The thatched roof was supported by a timber beam, and when Creswell Heritage Trust moved from its old visitor centre to the new one in May 2009, this timber support beam was discovered amongst their varied collection of archaeological artefacts. It had been placed in storage and largely forgotten about, but measures are now being considered to preserve and perhaps display this artefact. This little story is one of many that can be told by the artefacts discovered here at the Crags and all paint a wonderful picture about its rich history. But it is not medieval water mills that the Crags are famous for, it is its Palaeolithic (Old Stone Age) caves.

I.1 – *Location of Creswell Crags* (M. Beresford)

I.2 – George Stubbs' 'Two Gentlemen Going a shooting, with a view of Creswell Crags, Taken on the Spot', c. 1767, oil on canvas (Public Domain)

These caves harboured one of the richest collections of Palaeolithic occupation known in Britain, and have since proven to be one of the most northerly sites that Ice Age Man visited. Indeed, in 2003, we discovered that it is also the home of Britain's only known Ice Age cave art. But that is another story. This book attempts to pull all of those stories together and document who those Ice Age people were that used the Crags, what they were doing there and how, over time, archaeologists have pieced together the thousands of pieces of the puzzle in order to understand this.

Much has been written on the archaeology and history of Creswell Crags, but these tend to be isolated approaches or rather dated. We are lacking an up-to-date work that gathers all the information and attempts to put together a cohesive picture of the site, something which this book also aims to address.

The purpose of this book, then, is to investigate how past work and interpretations of the site have changed over time, and how these have invariably led to how the site has been managed and promoted. The first chapter aims to explore the early antiquarians and their work at Creswell in the 1870s and how they laid the foundations for future work. Chapter 2 then focuses on the more methodological approach of Alan Leslie Armstrong in the 1920s and 1930s when scientific methods were advancing and the archaeological techniques became more proficient. From these two chapters a specific picture of how Creswell was used in the past shall emerge, and ultimately led to the idea of a centralised system for Britain (known as the 'Creswellian') in the final stages of the Pleistocene, ultimately isolating it from its potential place in a wider European context. The discovery of what is essentially Magdalenian (or perhaps Magdalenian-inspired) art in Church Hole cave in 2003 revolutionised our thinking on this matter, and this is discussed in Chapter 3. Chapter 4 then examines how recent research has radically altered our view on the site and the Creswellian in general, before we then consider how all this information, and the newly discovered cave art, can be used to argue against Garrod's proposal of a localised British industry and reasserts Britain's place upon a much wider continental Palaeolithic map. This is discussed in Chapter 5, which also addresses the question of how the site should now be managed, promoted and used to educate, both the public and the academic world, in the present and in the future – essentially how Creswell Crags developed (and should continue to be developed) as a heritage site. The final chapter then looks at whether, from all this information, we can confidently ask 'who was Creswell Man?' and attempts to address the differences (or similarities) between the Neanderthal inhabitants and the Modern Humans. The work culminates by looking at what happened after the Last Ice Age and how the land, and settlement patterns, altered in this period.

In 1926, after fifty years of work at Creswell Crags, the archaeologist Dorothy Garrod coined the term the Creswellian for what she suggested as a localised British industry in the Late Upper Palaeolithic. In doing this she severed the links between Britain and its European neighbours. Some eighty years later I would challenge that view. Garrod chose the site of Creswell Crags as her type-site for her 'Creswellian' model on the basis that the flint assemblage discovered there, predominantly shouldered points and backed blades, showed such an abundance in variety that it was a superlative in representing the uniqueness of a British culture.[1] Jacobi, however, recently stressed the point that it was exactly due to this wide variety that Creswell should *not* be used as a definitive model.[2]

There is human occupation evidence at Creswell from around 60,000 years ago up to the present day and much of this early period, along with later occupation evidence, is discussed over the course of this book. As far as actual historical interest in the gorge goes, we had to wait until the latter half of the 19th century, when cave exploration became quite popular. Prior to this the intrepid antiquarians focused their attention on the burial mounds, which we now know date to later Prehistory, namely the Neolithic and Bronze Ages. The thought process behind this was based on the idea put forward in the Bible that the world was created in precisely 4004BC, and the antiquarian explorers took this as gospel (no pun intended!). They therefore set out to find the 'Ancient Britons' of the period, and soon discovered their remains in the barrows and tumuli littering the landscape.[3] But with the publication, and consequent acceptance by the scientific world, of Charles Darwin's theories on evolution (*On the Origin of Species,* 1859) society soon realised that our earliest ancestors went much, much further back in time. These ideas were applied to early discoveries by the Rev. William Buckland such as the Palaeolithic burial of the 'Red Lady' at Paviland Cave on the Gower Peninsula and of extinct animal bones at the cave site of Kirkdale, Yorkshire, both in the early 1820s.

Initially, Buckland believed that the deposits of sand and gravels within the caves he explored were evidence of the great flood (Darwin's theories would later challenge and disprove Buckland's 'great flood' hypothesis). Much like the Rev. J Magens Mello would discover in his later exploration at Creswell, Kirkdale Cave showed evidence of animal

---

[1] Dorothy Garrod *The Upper Palaeolithic Age in Britain,* (Oxford), 1926
[2] Roger Jacobi *The Creswellian, Creswell and Cheddar,* in *The Late Glacial in north-west Europe: human adaptation and environmental change at the end of the Pleistocene,* Barton, N, Roberts, A J and Roe, D A (eds), CBA Research Report No. 77, 1991, pp. 128-40
[3] For an account of local antiquarian barrow-digging, see Thomas Bateman's *Vestiges of the Antiquities of Derbyshire* (1848) which details his work in the Peak District

1.3 – Timber support beam from the medieval wooden mill at Creswell Crags (M. Beresford)

bones being gnawed by hyaenas leading Buckland to suggest it to be an early hyaena den. He became so obsessed by this that he decided to experiment with a live hyaena to attempt to understand how they ate the bones and how they subsequently regurgitated them. Initially, he borrowed one from a travelling circus but eventually purchased his own – his intention was to kill it and dissect its stomach, but in the end he had grown so attached to 'Billy', as he fondly named it, that he could not bring himself to do this and ended up keeping him as a pet for nigh on twenty-five years![4]

His experiments showed that hyaenas bit off large fragments from the upper part of a bone using their molar teeth and swallowed them whole. On retrieving the fragments

---

[4] Chris Stringer *Homo Brittanicus*, (London), 2006

I.4 – *William Buckland (1784-1856)* (Public Domain)

Buckland compared them to Palaeolithic remains of bison bones from Kirkdale Cave, noting the same tell-tale marks on these remains as those from his own experiments. William Boyd Dawkins, who dug with Mello at Creswell (see Chapter 1), was a noted admirer of Buckland's work, and commented on the hyaena experiments in his own work, *Cave-Hunting* (1874), which detailed his varying beliefs on the study of caves and undoubtedly shaped his methods at Creswell.

These new theories and the recent discoveries led the antiquarians to begin the systematic study of cave sites and consequently led Mello to obtain permission to explore the Creswell caves in the mid-1870s (see Chapter 1), principally, on the Derbyshire side, Mother Grundy's Parlour (named, legend informs us, as Old Mother Grundy – a local 'witch' or herbalist – lived there for a time in the 19th century), Robin Hood Cave (the outlaw is said to have escaped the Sheriff's men by hiding in the cave) and Pin Hole (Victorian ladies dropped hat pins into a recess in the cave in order to bring good luck) and on the Nottinghamshire side Church Hole (no one is quite sure how this name came about, but it could simply be due to the roof of the cave mirroring that of a church ceiling).

These early restraints within the scientific world are reflected by Mello himself when he commented how *'some forty years* (from 1879) *or so ago the possibility of man having been a contemporary of the mammalian fauna of the Pleistocene was, if not openly*

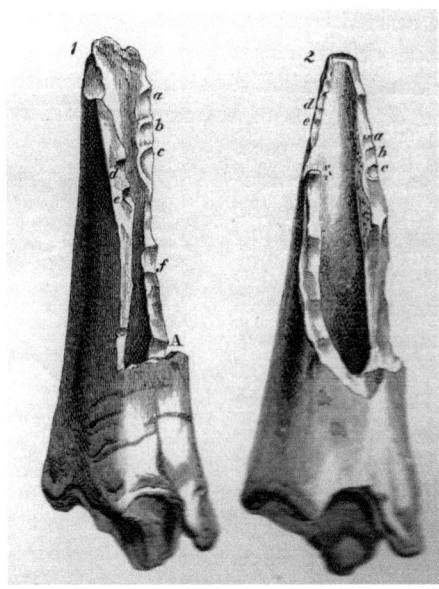

I.5 – *Leg bones gnawed by hyaenas, with similarities labelled, (left) Buckland's experimental bone, (right) bone of bison from Kirkdale (Public Domain)*

derided, yet received with great scepticism, even in the scientific world'.[5] Nevertheless, the results were astounding.

Cornelius Brown offered his view on Creswell and the early exploration in 1896:

> 'The most picturesque exposure of the magnesian limestone in Nottinghamshire is at Creswell Crags, near Worksop. Here time and a running stream have carved out and fashioned a long ravine. On each side of the stream in the tall limestone cliffs are deep caverns, which have recently been explored by a committee of the British Association. In these caverns have been found an amazing number of remains of animals long ago extinct in this country. Amongst these were the lion, tiger, leopard, hyena, wolf, bear, rhinoceros, bison, hippopotamus, Arctic fox, and the elephant. Doubtless the Creswell caves were in ages past the abode of the cave-dwelling hyenas who dragged their prey into these recesses in the rock. A large proportion of the bones found were gnawed after the manner peculiar to the hyena tribe. In one of these caves the writer discovered a 'first milk molar' of the mammoth (Elephas primigenius), which completed the national collection of the teeth of the mammoth. Before this specimen was handed over to the British Museum, it was described by Sir Richard Owen, F.R.S., before the Geological Society of London. A portion of Creswell Crags is in Derbyshire, but the magnesian limestone of that spot is a totally distinct rock from the 'mountain limestone,' which is such a familiar feature in the scenery of Derbyshire.'[6]

By the turn of the century the importance of the discoveries at Creswell were being wholly realised, particularly because the Midlands, and indeed Britain, were unable to offer up anything remotely close to Mello and his compatriots' discoveries. The *Victoria County History* informs us of this local scarcity: '*the Pleistocene deposits of Derbyshire*

---

[5] Rev. J Magens Mello *Palaeolithic Man at Creswell, Derbyshire Archaeological Journal,* Vol. I, 1879
[6] Cornelius Brown *A History of Nottinghamshire* (1896)

I.6 – *Aerial view of Creswell Crags*
(© Creswell Heritage Trust)

are comparatively meagre…(as opposed to the Trent basin) (but) *a few of these deposits have yielded remains; but the smallness of the number is remarkable, owing perhaps to only a few of the caverns* (being) *excavated'.*[7] When the work was published in 1905 it deemed it 'remarkable' that nothing had been found in the Carboniferous Limestone (ie.

---

[7] *Victoria County History,* Vol. I, (London), 1905 p. 163

the Peak District) and that only the recent discoveries at Kent's Hole, Torquay surpassed those made by Mello at Creswell, a telling testament to the importance of the site.

In his study of the Late Upper Palaeolithic (on which period this work focuses) Campbell[8] suggested that the cultural material of the period was directly concentrated in these cave sites, particularly along the 'contact zones between highlands and lowlands' – as is the case at Creswell – and that this most likely represented the ancient hunting practice of exploiting 'two or more viable environmental zones at the same time for greater economic yield'.[9] So what was this 'environmental zone' at Creswell like in the Late Upper Palaeolithic? Campbell describes it thus:

> *'The Late Upper Palaeolithic is associated with a Late Last Glacial environment varying between Boreal and Sub-Arctic. The flora is that of a nearly treeless steppe-tundra, with shrubby forms of Juniper, Willow and Birch, and, particularly during Zone II, occasional coppices of tree birches. The fauna suggests similar conditions and its land mammals include notably brown bear, woolly rhinoceros, wild horse, red deer, giant deer and reindeer, the main food animals again being wild horse and reindeer'.*[10]

This description gives us a good idea of what the landscape was like at Creswell in the period and can go someway to aid us in our understanding of why Palaeolithic man was drawn to the caves. It is a marked contrast to the picture of Creswell today: 'Creswell Crags is found today amidst a decaying industrial conurbation, a landscape that could hardly be more different from the beauty of ice-age tundra'.[11] This view is a little harsh, and recent developments in the area have improved it considerably, but one gets the point. So this book shall focus on understanding the Palaeolithic history of Creswell Crags and attempt to address the question as to whether Garrod's view of a localised British industry is still applicable, whilst also questioning whether because of this Creswell is finally realising its potential as a forerunner in being one of Britain's, and indeed Europe's, premier Palaeolithic visitor sites.

---

[8] J B Campbell *The Upper Palaeolithic of Britain,* (Oxford), 1977, p. 412
[9] Ibid.
[10] Ibid.
[11] Steve Mithen *After the Ice: A Global Human History, 20,000-5000BC,* (London), 2003, p. 118

1
Antiquarian Interest & Early Fieldwork

1.1 – *The Reverend J Magens Mello (1836-1914)* (Public Domain)

During the final part of the 19th century some of the Creswell Caves were being used as cattle byres. Documentary evidence of Church Hole cave, on the Nottinghamshire side of the gorge, of a retaining wall approximately 20ft into the cave supports this notion. One might suppose that this coming and going of the cows and the consequent rubbing against the cave walls would have had a detrimental impact on the archaeology and history of the cave deposits. However, what this disturbance revealed was a tooth, later identified as mammoth, found in one of the caves by a labourer known only to us as 'Woodhead'.[1] Even the exact cave itself remains unclear, but it is most likely to have been one of the larger caves, perhaps Robin Hood Cave or Church Hole.

The tooth was sent for analysis where it was confirmed as being mammoth, and Mr Frank Tebbet (Superintendent of Creswell Quarries), Dr. Bergener (of Worksop) and Mr Bailey (of Mansfield) carried out a number of surveys at the Crags between 1870-73.[2] They found further mammoth teeth along with the tooth of a rhinoceros, but all were surface finds and up to this point no excavations were carried out. The following

---

[1] J. Magens Mello *On some bone-caves in Creswell Crags,* Report to the Geological Society, (1875)
[2] Ibid. (1875)

year, in 1874, the Reverend J Magens Mello applied for permission to carry out the first excavations at a cave known at the time as 'Fissure C' (probably Church Hole, although this is still uncertain). This exploration was subsequently abandoned due to a 'blocking wall' – could this be the wall mentioned above built to retain cattle in the Church Hole cave? Permission was also obtained to carry out work at 'Fissure A' (Pin Hole) and 'Cavern B' (Robin Hood Cave) with a Mr White and a team of workmen assisting Mello.

Mello himself was born in London and received some schooling in Paris, becoming a member of the Sociètè Scientifiquè de Bruxelles and an Honorary Member of the Burton Archaeological and Natural History Society. He was also curate for a time at All Saint's Church in Derby, before becoming Rector of the Church of St. Thomas, New Brampton, in 1863, where he served for 25 years. Thus he would have been familiar with the area and would have known of Creswell Crags prior to his work there.

In his report to the Geological Society in 1875 he explained his initial interest in the site:

> *'Some years ago I had formed a strong wish to examine the fissures in this locality, but until lately could never find the opportunity. Last April (1874), however, I was enabled...a very brief inspection...*(which) *sufficed to show me that it was one well worth careful exploration'.*[3]

Mello further detailed how he had found the leg bone of a rhinoceros about '3 or 4 inches below the surface' in Fissure C, and that although the first three days in Fissure A (Pin Hole) had proven unfruitful he finally came upon an underlying bed of red sand that proved to be 'rich in bones'. Many of these bones had been gnawed by hyaenas, of which numerous teeth and jaw fragments were found, suggesting that the Pin Hole may well have been an early hyaena den. Also present amongst the Pin Hole bones were a number of examples of the water vole *Arvicola terrestris cantiana*. In the present *Arvicola* bones can be used to date a site using the 'vole clock' based on the principle that early Palaeolithic sites within Europe, such as Gran Dolina in Spain (circa. 780,000BC), reflect evidence of the more primitive water vole *Mimomys savini* and later sites, such as Boxgrove in Sussex, have *Arvicola*. What this means for Creswell is that it fits into a much later European context, although Mello and his team could not have known this at the time given the scientific methods and principles of the period. Chris Stringer, of the Ancient Human Occupation of Britain team (AHOB) explains the 'vole clock' thus: *'the vole clock is based on the evolutionary transition between the primitive and extinct vole called Mimomys savini and the water vole Arvicola terrestris cantiana. Mimomys had molar teeth with closed roots, whereas the molars of its descendant, Arvicola, are open-rooted and ever growing'.*[4]

In Cavern B (Robin Hood Cave) Mello noted that it had 'evidently been used for human occupation' – as well as the presence once more of rhino and hyaena teeth. There were also discovered a number of flint chippings, part of a flint flake and 'some implements made of pebbles' (here, Mello means Quartzite, a raw material derived locally from the Bunter Sandstones). And this was pretty much all that Mello could deduce from his first season of excavations. What is interesting to add at this point, taken from Professor Busk's report on the animal bones from the 1874 season (included in Mello's report of 1875), is the wide variety of animals present within the Crags. These included bear, hyaena, wolf, fox, arctic fox, bovine, reindeer, Irish elk, sheep, horse, rhino, mammoth

---

[3] Ibid, p.679
[4] Chris Stringer *Homo Britannicus*, (Bury St Edmunds), 2006, p.41

and vole. Busk's interpretation of the data suggested that, regarding the hyaena, the remains appeared to belong to 'aged individuals' given that some of the teeth had literally worn down to stumps.[5] Busk also discussed the presence of both arctic and English varieties of the fox, noting the arctic fox to be considerably smaller and that to his knowledge the Creswell example was at that point the only known example of the continental arctic fox in Britain.[6]

The following year, in 1875, Mello returned to Creswell along with Frank Tebbet and Thomas Heath of Derby Museum. Once more they excavated in Pin Hole but it appears could make no further progress in this cave, indeed Heath only mentions their work in Pin Hole fleetingly: *'Early in the following July (1875), I began to assist Mr. Mello. After working out the Pin Hole, we began in what is called Robin Hood Cave'.*[7] Indeed, in their joint paper in 1880 *On the exploration of Creswell Crags* Mello and Heath summarised Pin Hole as being 'a mere fissure' some 40 or 50 yards long, and although it contained a large number of animal bones these were frequently found matted together, often with 4 or 5 bones of different animals found in close contact. They surmised the cave had most likely been victim to ice flow and wash and that the artefacts within had been shifted and re-arranged thus.[8] Further to this they only discovered one example of flint, hence the hyaena den interpretation. What is interesting is that they noted the presence of Glutton (or Wolverine) and commented that there was little previous evidence of this in Britain but considerable evidence in Belgium. This could then be seen as possible evidence to support later theories on migratory patterns in an East-West direction, as opposed to South-North.

The work in Robin Hood Cave revealed animal bones in the form of rhino, a jaw and four canines of hyaena, the lower jaw, tarsus, metacarpal and humerus of Irish elk, and also the incisor of a human. Heath stated that the bones showed no sign of gnawing, which perhaps supports the 'human occupation' theory of the previous season, and differs somewhat in use to that of Pin Hole. In fact, generally, the fauna of the two caves is markedly similar, but there are considerably more in the line of flint and quartzite tools present in Robin Hood Cave. The stratigraphy also proved more complex than that of Pin Hole, but it is important to note that all but the deepest layer contained organic remains (ie. animal bones).[9] Mello and Heath concluded from their research on the two caves that the fauna is on the whole identical but that each had certain animals missing based on the other. As far as the excavation in Robin Hood Cave itself was concerned, the workers encountered a layer of limestone breccia that proved 'intensely hard' and needed 'frequent blasting', but that this layer contained flint tools which included examples of 'carefully wrought lanceolate weapons'[10] similar to those from Solutrè and other French cave sites and similar to Belgian cave sites. Below this breccia layer they noted that the flint tools were far less elaborate and that quartzite tools were also present. They suggested these flint tools may have been of Mousterian (Neanderthal) type and may be similar to those found in the lowest levels of Kent's Cavern in southern Britain (which Mello also excavated). Below this they noted the same red sand that was present in Pin Hole and again was void of human evidence.

In 1876 William Boyd Dawkins was added to the excavation team (see Appendix for his account of the tools required for cave-digging), and the survey of Robin Hood Cave

---

[5] Professor Busk's report in Mello *On some bone-caves*, 1875, p. 683
[6] Ibid, p. 686
[7] Thomas Heath *Pleistocene deposits of Derbyshire*, in *Derbyshire Archaeological Journal*, Volume IV, 1882, p. 171
[8] Mello & Heath *On the exploration of Creswell caves*, 1880
[9] Ibid, p. 107
[10] Ibid, p. 108

was completed and further work undertaken in Church Hole. His opinion on the results of this final season in Robin Hood Cave was that they were *'of considerable importance, not merely because they confirm the conclusions which were arrived at from the previous explorations, but because they add new facts to the history of Palaeolithic Man in Britain'.*[11]

1.2 – *Sir William Boyd Dawkins (1837-1929)* (Public Domain)

Returning for the moment to the red sand and clay deposits that compare in both Pin Hole and Robin Hood Cave (and are deemed hyaena den deposits) it is interesting to note that they appear to reflect a scarcer faunal population. The ratio pointed out by Boyd Dawkins is 156 individual finds in the red sand deposit compared to 3610 finds in the later breccia and cave-earth deposits. This coincides with the 'no human occupation' evidence below the cave-earth. Now, it was noted by Boyd Dawkins in 1877 that the bone remains were less gnawed and in better condition in the red sand than those from within the cave-earth. Also, that 8 flints were discovered in the red sand but 1032 in the cave-earth.

The conclusions that Boyd Dawkins came to (and no doubt Mello and Heath also) were not that far from the truth. That the 'rude implements of quartzite' were used before the more 'carefully finished implements of flint' is without doubt. In the present, and largely through tool analysis, we are aware that the quartzite artefacts date to the Neanderthals or Middle Palaeolithic (around 60-45,000 years ago at Creswell) and therefore the archaeology of this early antiquarian period supports the argument. The hyaena den must, therefore, predate the Middle Palaeolithic, and that all the tools in the red sand were quartzite has to suggest that the red sand deposit / earliest human occupation must be Middle Palaeolithic.

Also during the 1876 season two hugely important artefacts were discovered in Robin Hood Cave. Both caused much controversy and debate, and yet are integral to our understanding of the site and its place within a wider European context. Firstly, let us consider the image of a horse engraved on a horse rib bone found by Mello in July 1876, which Boyd Dawkins describes as being *'the most important discovery of the handiwork of man...the head and forequarters of a horse incised on a smoothed and rounded fragment of a rib, cut short off at one end and broken at the other'.*[12] He also pointed out of similar known examples from the Continent at Perigord (France) and Kesslerloch (Switzerland). However, Heath furiously argued that the art was a forgery and had been placed there by persons unknown. Boyd Dawkins countered these claims by stating that he had been present when Mello found the piece and that Heath had not. What followed was a series of accusations and counter-claims by the parties involved. In a letter to the *Manchester City News* John Plant argued that *'there is no dispute about this object on either side. It is admitted to be identical in colour, style and feature with similar engraved pieces of bone* (to those from France or Italy)*...there is no such thing yet known as a piece of bone bearing marks of intelligible ideas or natural forms from any Pleistocene deposit in the*

---

[11] William Boyd Dawkins *On the mammal fauna of Creswell Caves*, (1877)
[12] Ibid, p.592

1.3 – *Robin Hood Cave during the 19th century excavations*
(© Creswell Heritage Trust)

1.4 – *Artefacts from the 19th century excavations at Creswell*
(© Creswell Heritage Trust)

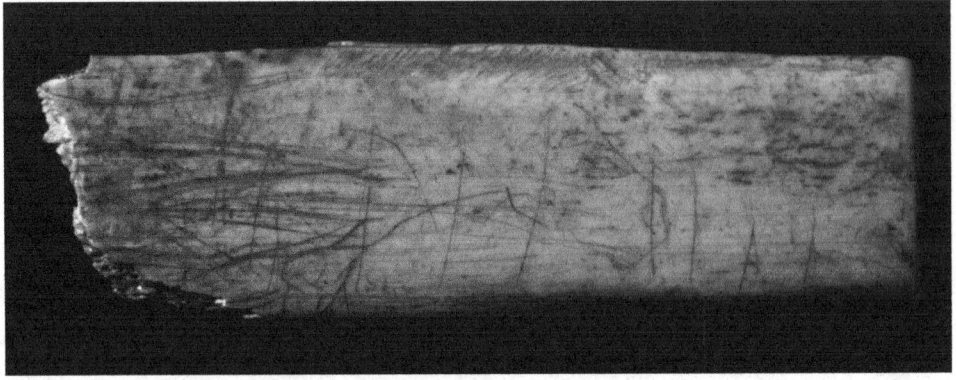

*1.5 – The horse engraving from Robin Hood Cave
(© Creswell Heritage Trust)*

British Isles'.[13] As Bahn[14] quite rightly argues just because no previous portable art had been discovered in Britain, did that alone mean the Creswell art had to be a plant? Its authenticity was not disputed, we must note, just its genuineness as an archaeological deposit within the Creswell caves.

The debate raged on and prompted W G Sollas in his 1924 book *Ancient Hunters and their Modern Representatives* to claim that *'there is a singular absence of any attempt at art in all the Palaeolithic stations of England. The horse here is, I am assured, a forgery introduced into the cave by a mischievous person'*.[15] Once again Boyd Dawkins was quick to counter, claiming that Sollas had informed him the Rev. Mullins of Langwith Bassett had spoken with him (Sollas) on the matter and stated the piece was a forgery. Boyd Dawkins thus argues that the forgery claim was merely based on hearsay and was without tangible proof. Whether this was actually the case or not, Sollas later omitted the claim from his book.

It could be suggested, however, that the portable art was indeed genuine and was discovered in Robin Hood Cave legitimately, but that its reputation was tarnished by the second questionable discovery made in the *same* cave, in the *same* deposit just four days later. This time the find in question was the tooth of the *Machairodus* (scimitar toothed cat) found by Boyd Dawkins himself: *'the discovery of the incised drawing of a palaeolithic horse is rivalled in value by that of the rare animal Machairodus in the same stratum at a short distance away'*.[16] He further believed that it was quite similar to that found in Kent's Hole in Britain and to one he had examined from Chagny, nr Dijon, at the Museum of Lyons, and that it proved that the *Machairodus* was living in France but also in Britain and was a *'survival from the Pliocene into the Pleistocene age'*[17] much like the woolly rhino, horse and mammoth (based on the Creswell and Kent's Hole examples).

Analysis of the tooth, admittedly by Boyd Dawkins himself, suggested it had been introduced by the 'hand of man' in that it appeared to have been broken off by a sharp blow. There was no evidence to suggest any gnawing by hyaenas, and there may be evidence of a few scratches made by flint at its base. It could, quite feasibly, be argued

---

[13] Quoted in Heath, *Creswell caves vs Professor Boyd Dawkins*, 1880, p. 22
[14] Paul Bahn *Historical background to Discovery of Cave Art*, in Pettitt, Bahn & Ripoll *Palaeolithic cave art at Creswell Crags in wider European context*, (Oxford, 2007)
[15] W G Sollas *Ancient Hunters and their Modern Representatives*, 1924, footnote, p. 536
[16] Boyd Dawkins On the mammal fauna, p. 594
[17] Ibid, p. 594

Species	Total from both deposits	Grey sand	Red sand and clay					Breccia and cave earth				
			Jaws	Teeth	Bones, antlers	Tools	Total	Jaws	Teeth	Bones, antlers	Tools	Total
1. Man (*Homo*)	1040					8	8				1032	1032
2. *Machairodus latidens*	1								1			1
3. Lion (var. *Felis spelaea*)	10								2	8		10
4. Wild Cat (*F. catus*)	3							3				3
5. Leopard (*F. pardus*)	1									1		1
6. Spotted Hyaena (var. *H. spelaea*)	928		4	32	4		40	49	780	59		888
7. Fox (*Canis vulpes*)	121		9	4			13	30	27	51		108
8. Wolf (*C. lupus*)	61							1	28	32		61
9. Bear	78							2	39	37		78
10. Reindeer (*C. tarandus*)	473			20	12		32	1	180	260		441
11. Irish elk (*C. megaceros*)	18			3	1		5	6	7			13
12. Bison (var. *Bison priscus*)	20			1			1		10	9		19
13. Horse (*Equus caballus*)	550			22	25		49	1	490	10		501
14. Woolly rhinoceros (*R. tichorhinus*)	357			3			3		250	104		354
15. Mammoth (*Elephas primigenius*)	53			2	2		4		46	3		49
16. Hare (*Lepus timidus*)	52			2	1		1			51		51
Totals	3766						156					3610

1.6 - Pleistocene fauna of Robin Hood Cave (adapted from Boyd Dawkins, 1876)

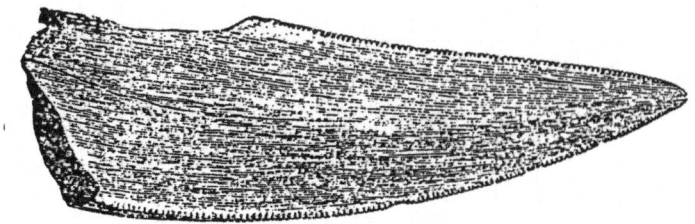

1.7 – 1920s image of the upper canine of Machairodus from Robin Hood Cave (bottom) compared to a modern tiger tooth (above) (© Creswell Heritage Trust)

once again that much like the portable 'horse' art it could have been brought to Creswell from somewhere else, and that this could even have occurred in Palaeolithic times, so does not necessarily reflect, even if genuine, the *Machairodus* being native to Britain. Yet again, Boyd Dawkins had an answer for this. Although fossil collecting, he argued, was quite prevalent from the period and examples did appear in the archaeological record (for example in the Museum of Florence, from the Val d'Arno), these examples date to the Pliocene.[18]

The final say on the matter from the point of view of its origin can be left to science, as analysis of the tooth later revealed that the mineral condition of the Creswell tooth suggests that it is in fact local – examples from the Continent are of a differing colour variation and preservation condition. In a letter in *Nature* dated December 4th 1879 from Boyd Dawkins we hear that:

> *'it is insinuated (by Thomas Heath) that the engraved bone (discovered by Mello) and the tooth of the Machairodus are not <u>bona fide</u> discoveries…but were placed there by some one, not specified, and were derived from some other locality.'*[19]

He further argues that, regarding Mello's discovery, Heath was not present whilst he was and can authenticate the discovery. Yet Heath appeared more concerned with Boyd Dawkins' discovery of the tooth, arguing that the tooth was 'without adherent matrix' and 'without the moisture which it would possess had it been embedded in the cave for ages'.[20] Boyd Dawkins countered this be stating the claims were false, the tooth had split in pieces upon drying and that the red-earth (the matrix alluded to by Heath) was still visible in the pulp cavity. He finished his letter by attacking Heath, describing him as 'not a member of the Exploration Committee' and being 'merely a subordinate to Mr Mello' and that he held back his findings and notes deemed by himself (that is Heath) to be valuable for nearly three years. Mello backed up his colleague's opinion: *'the presence of that formidable animal the Machairodus, in Derbyshire and the adjoining counties, appears probable from the presence of one of its teeth, the condition of which is perfectly similar to that of the teeth of the other animals found in the caves'.*[21] Unperturbed,

---

[18] Ibid, p. 595
[19] William Boyd Dawkins, *Nature,* Dec. 4th 1879
[20] Ibid, 1879
[21] J Magens Mello *Palaeolithic Man at Creswell*, 1879, p.21

Heath concluded his own article on Creswell, *Pleistocene Deposits of Derbyshire* (1882) thus: '*I have deliberately omitted Machairodus latideus because of the impossibility of its really belonging to the Creswell fauna, as stated by professor Boyd Dawkins, since the reasons there adduced have been sufficient to justify Dr. Geikie in omitting it from his work, Prehistoric Europe'.*[22] A final point worth noting from Boyd Dawkins' 1877 report is that of the 200 reindeer teeth found within Robin Hood Cave, eleven of them were milk-molars which testifies to the presence of young deer and this is important as it may suggest that reindeer young were hunted as well as the adults.

Also in the 1876 season work again focussed on Church Hole cave. Here it was found that the cave deposits and associated finds were markedly similar to those of Robin Hood Cave, although within the red sand layer finds were more abundant and yet were rather fragmentary. The hypothesis here was that hyaenas must have been more prominent in Church Hole during the earlier stages of occupation.

Essentially the stratigraphy of Church Hole revealed that in the deposits above the red sand layer fragments of charcoal and calcined bone were present, although the lower levels were once again markedly similar to Robin Hood Cave: in the lower deposits were found a few crude quartzite implements and in the upper deposits artefacts of bone, antler and flint. The bone and antler artefacts are worth considering at this point as they are integral to our understanding of the purpose of the cave:

1) A well-shaped needle made from a metacarpal or tarsal bone. Interestingly, this is larger than contemporary examples from France, Belgium and Switzerland.

1.8 – Replica of the bone needle from Church Hole with animal gut thread
(M. Beresford)

2) 2 bone awls made from the tibia of a hare.

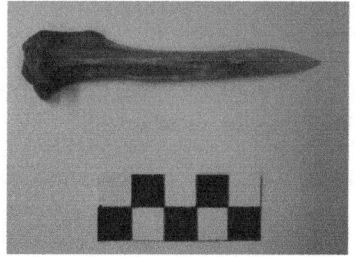

1.9 – Replica of the bone awl from Church Hole
(M. Beresford)

---

[22] Thomas Heath *Pleistocene Deposits of Derbyshire, Derbyshire Archaeological Journal,* Volume IV, 1882, p. 178

3) A broad, spatulate fragment made from the distal portion of the transverse process of one of the lumbar vertebrae most likely of 'horse or large ruminant'.[23] Boyd Dawkins believed that it closely resembled a similar piece from the Grotte de lá Gorge d'Enfer although the Church Hole example had rather deeper notches and these were spaced further apart.

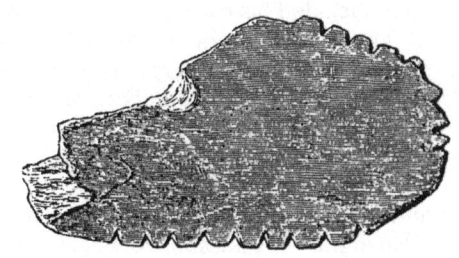

1.10 – *Notched bone from Church Hole cave* (© Creswell Heritage Trust)

4) 2 antler rods, both broken and perhaps being examples of spear-heads. Once again, they were noted as being markedly similar to Continental examples such as the spear-heads from Kesslerloch, Switzerland.

It was suggested in the 1877 report that the condition of the fossil remains at Creswell, ie. bones, antler and teeth, could be put into three separate groups:

- those that had been gnawed by hyaenas
- those that been broken, or burnt, by man
- those that had been attacked by carbonic acids in the rainwater that had percolated through the cave-earth and red sand deposits

In summary, Robin Hood Cave and Church Hole had been inhabited at the same time and the fauna was alike in both. This fauna belonged to a group that had spread over Central Europe from the Pyrenées as far north as the Elbe, and 'swung to and fro' according to the season.[24] Generally it was believed that they would follow the route from the low-grazing land now under the 'German Ocean' (North Sea – ie. Doggerland) up to the line of the Trent to Creswell. As Boyd Dawkins believed *'the Pleistocene fauna is not divided from that which went before and that which followed after by a barrier of ice. The Palaeolithic hunters of the Creswell Caves, judged by the geological standard, belong to the late Pleistocene age, since the numerous remains of reindeer prove that the Arctic mammalia were then in the possession of the land'.*[25]

This was to be the end of the exploration into Creswell's caves but in 1877 the tooth of a hippopotamus was discovered in Mother Grundy's Parlour. The tooth, conveniently 'acquired' by Messrs. Duffy and Gain, was purchased by a Mr John Young who noted that in the previous excavations undertaken at Creswell no fauna from notable warmer climatic periods (ie. inter-glacial) had been discovered. One can assume that the prospect of finding evidence for this was sorely tempting for Boyd Dawkins and his compatriots and they not surprisingly opted to carry out excavations in the cave. As

---

[23] Boyd Dawkins *On the mammal fauna*, p. 604
[24] Boyd Dawkins *On the mammal fauna*, p. 606
[25] Boyd Dawkins *On the mammal fauna*, p. 611

	Total from both deposits	Red sand					Stalagmitic Breccias and Cave earth				
		Jaws	Teeth	Bones, antlers	Tools	Total	Jaws	Teeth	Bones, antlers	Tools	Total
1. Man (*Homo*)	234				23	23				211	211
2. Lion (var. *Felis spelaea*)	2								2		2
3. Polecat (*M. putorius*)	1	1				1					
4. Spotted Hyaena (var. *H. spelaea*)	410	13	140	32		185	33	144	48		225
5. Fox (*Canis vulpes*)	19		2			2	10	1	6		17
6. Wolf (*C. lupus*)	19	4	3			7	3	2	7		12
7. Bear	55		10	12		22		10	23		33
8. Reindeer (*C. tarandus*)	412	37		101		138	8	55	211		274
9. Irish elk (*C. megaceros*)	14	2	4	3		9	1	2	2		5
10. Bison (var. *Bison priscus*)	45			11		11	3	6	25		34
11. Horse (*Equus caballus*)	310		90	30		120	1	170	19		190
12. Woolly rhinoceros (*R. tichorhinus*)	250		31	70		101	2	51	96		149
13. Mammoth (*Elephas primigenius*)	57		10	8		18		33	6		39
14. Hare (*Lepus timidus*)	10		2			2			8		8
Totals	1838	57	292	267	23	639	61	474	453	211	1199

1.11 – *Pleistocene fauna of Church Hole Cave* (M. Beresford, Source: Boyd Dawkins, 1876)

Boyd Dawkins explained,[26] at the time it was initially deemed 'not to be worthwhile due to past treasure-hunting' but that after John Young showed them the hippo tooth (which was so obviously different to all the previously discovered 'arctic fauna') they decided to explore the cave.

The areas investigated by the team were the main chamber and the first half of the smaller passageway. The main chamber had a surface soil with fragments of charcoal, burnt clay and bones and a number of flint chips with a few flint flakes. The team deemed it to be equivalent in date to the 'superficial layer' found in both Robin Hood Cave and Church Hole. Then came a layer of a red, sandy cave-earth housing animal remains of bison, reindeer, bear, wolf, fox and hyaena (interestingly, hyaena coprolites were numerous and had been preserved by the dryness of the cave). What this suggested was that Mother Grundy's Parlour may not have been subjected to the disturbance from glacial waters as Robin Hood Cave had been. They also noted a few quartzite pebbles, and curiously a few flint flakes in the very upper part of this layer, although it seems likely that these may have come in fact from the layer above. Finally, they noted a red clay and ferruginous sand deposit that contained skull fragments and other bones of hippo, rhino teeth, hyaena skulls and jaws and remains of bison.

In the passageway there was again a layer of the red, sandy cave-earth and again bones and teeth of bison, reindeer, hyaena and bear were present. However, on the north side of this area, approximately 19ft from the entrance a human skull was discovered. In close proximity were the vertebra of bison and quartzite splinters. Boyd Dawkins' assessment was that it was most likely much later in date, and in this he may have been correct as we shall see in the next chapter. Finally, the red clay layer was evident and again contained remains of hyaena, bison, hippo and rhino, but no human implements.

The most striking point to note from this stratigraphy (aside from the much earlier faunal remains) is that the breccia and upper cave-earth deposit, with the finer flint tools and gnawed bones, present in both Robin Hood Cave and Church Hole is missing from Mother Grundy's Parlour. Instead we see a correlation between the red, sandy cave-earth of Mother Grundy's Parlour and the red sand of Robin Hood Cave and Church Hole; that is they all appear to reflect the same period of prehistory. The quartzite pebbles and the preserved bones with no evidence of hyaena gnawing are evident in all three caves which would suggest a relatively earlier phase within Creswell's history. It is, however, curious to note that horse is well-represented in Robin Hood Cave and Church Hole and yet almost missing entirely from Mother Grundy's Parlour (save for 2 teeth) whilst bison remains are the complete opposite – abundant in Mother Grundy's Parlour yet scarce in Robin Hood Cave and Church Hole. What can be deduced from this then is that the red, sandy cave-earth of Mother Grundy's Parlour is the equivalent of the oldest stratum in the other two caves; the underlying red-sand and ferruginous sand reflects an even older period not represented in the other caves.

If we now consider the mammal fauna within these older deposits we can note a very different faunal make-up for the area based on evidence from the other caves. Spotted hyaena, fox, bear and bison are common to all but hippo and rhino are exclusive to Mother Grundy's Parlour and yet horse, woolly rhino and mammoth, and perhaps most importantly man, are missing (from the antiquarian excavations). The few implements that were present in the cave – a few pot boilers and splinters of quartzite, and one 'imperfect hache of ironstone of the *type Acheulian* similar to that from Robin Hood Cave'[27] – point to an early use, most likely Middle Palaeolithic.

---

[26] Dawkins & Mello *Further discoveries in the Creswell Caves*, 1879, p. 724
[27] Dawkins & Mello *Further discoveries*, 1879

The result of the time spent exploring the caves at Creswell led Boyd Dawkins, Mello & Co to suggest that at the time when the red clay and ferruginous sands were being deposited at Mother Grundy's Parlour, hippo, rhino, hyaena and bison inhabited the rather warm local area. There was, as yet, no sign of Palaeolithic man or the reindeer so important to later phases. Next, when the red sands were being deposited in all three caves mammoth, woolly rhino, horse and reindeer populated the area amidst an arctic climate. It was this period that was home to the earliest hunters of the locale, the Neanderthals with their quartzite tools. Finally, we see evidence for the 'Palaeolithic hunter' (notable in the breccia and cave-earth within Robin Hood Cave and Church Hole) – the flint tools similar to those from the Solutré, the bone and antler implements and a rare example of art in the form of the portable artwork of the horse incised on the rib bone, with Boyd Dawkins concluding that 'Creswell Man' had similar artistic faculties as his contemporaries in the south of France, Switzerland and Belgium.[28]

The early antiquarians certainly laid the foundations for the development of Creswell Crags as a heritage site, indeed their early, pioneering work is integral to our understanding of the site, and yet as time progressed into the twentieth century we began to realise that their work raised as many questions as it answered. Careful re-examination of the finds and more detailed field research shed fresh insight onto the caves and their role within Palaeolithic society and began to show that although the early work had got much of the history right, it had also got much of it wrong.

---

[28] Dawkins & Mello *Further discoveries*, 1879, p. 733

2
Armstrong's Research and Interpretations

> *'It is now 50 years since the Late Rev. J Magens Mello and Sir Wm. Boyd Dawkins startled the scientific world by proving that relics of humanity had been found in a cave at Creswell associated with remains of extinct animals'*
>
> Alan Leslie Armstrong, *The Pin Hole Cave,* 1926

In the autumn of 1924 work at Creswell Crags commenced once more. It is suggested that the period in between the then current excavations and those of the 1870s had been subjected to 'pot hunters and cave-diggers'[1] and further exploration of the caves was necessary in order to reveal a much clearer picture. The British Association for the Advancement of Science funded a series of excavations at Creswell Crags led by the archaeologist Alan Leslie Armstrong. The caves singled out by Armstrong were Pin Hole and Mother Grundy's Parlour, both of which had been examined, to an extent, by Mello, Dawkins and Co. The picture given by Armstrong was that his methods were much more stringent than the earlier work – for Pin Hole we hear '(it was) deemed advisable to excavate the cave in a series of sections 6-9ft in length. Each section examined in layers 6 to 12 inches thick, stripped off "like leaves from a writing pad", every particle of earth removed being passed through fine sieves'.[2] In all, 350 tons of earth were removed from the Pin Hole.

Armstrong's work revealed a stratigraphy of two beds of cave earth, an upper red layer and a lower yellow, with each having differing artefacts and faunal remains. An overlying stratum of black earth formed the cave floor, with Neolithic artefacts being the earliest datable material.

The upper cave earth had a faunal assemblage heavily dominated by reindeer, but also including Arctic fox and hare, woolly rhino, mammoth and horse. At a depth of 12 inches Armstrong recovered an engraved double bevel lance point of mammoth ivory, Magdalenian in design, which he described as indicating a 'definite correlation in time' for the cave earth and the middle Magdalenian in France. This did not suggest,

---

[1] A L Armstrong *The Pin Hole Cave,* Unpublished report to the British Association, 1926, p. 1
[2] Ibid, p.2

2.1 – *Alan Leslie Armstrong* (© Creswell Heritage Trust)

in Armstrong's opinion, that the inhabitants at Creswell and those of France's contemporary sites were the *same* people, just that there was evidence that 'establishes a definite contemporaniety between (the Magdalenian) and the distinctive culture of the upper Creswell'.[3] This is supported, according to Armstrong, by the fact that certain flints (namely shouldered points) from the 'mammoth ivory' layer in Pin Hole closely resemble other such flints from the lower portion of Mother Grundy's Parlour (also excavated by Armstrong and discussed shortly) and both these layers have a similar fauna. He deduced from this that the wider Continental Magdalenian element at Creswell was slight and was not a permanent influence, perhaps resulting from occasional visits by Magdalenian hunting parties.

This upper cave earth showed little evidence of any glacial inflow or mixing of deposits, as had been the case in some of the other caves, so Armstrong was able to suggest that the Aurignacian occupation must have been a long one with a relatively slow accumulation of deposition. The fauna present reflected a milder climate for the period with hot summers but severe winters. The lower portion of this layer was deemed to be Solutréan but again the influence was deemed slight and perhaps again reflected hunting parties. At the very base of the deposit the heavy presence of reindeer suggested a much colder climate and the evidence of quartzite hand-axes suggest the presence of 'Mousterian man' (Neanderthals). In the entrance passage notable occupation layers hinted at evidence of fires, but the relatively low amount of split bones and cooking stones led Armstrong to wonder whether this may be more representative of 'warning fires', that is as a deterrent to large carnivores, hyaenas for example, rather than hearths or cooking fires. Careful sieving revealed a multitude of small bones from animals such as voles, lemming, pole-cat, bats, birds and fish: clearly archaeological techniques were becoming far more stringent. This is further supported by the mammoth bone that was found with a flint blade lying between the flanges of the joint; Armstrong was taking his opportunity to excavate at Creswell very seriously indeed.

In the middle layers the fauna reflected reindeer, hyaena, horse and bear prominently. Flint artefacts included angle burins, Gravette, trapezoidal, Châtelperronian and Font Robert points, scrapers and blades. Armstrong also found a pierced shell bead and an oval shaped pendant from the tooth of a mammoth, a tiny bone awl and a larger specimen resembling a writing pen.[4] In the 'junction' between the upper and lower cave earths a number of Mousterian artefacts were noted which rather interestingly suggested that the Neanderthals, while being the last to occupy the cave just prior to the coming of the ice advance (within the Devensian cold stage), were also the first people to re-occupy the cave after its retreat. The lower cave earth, that is layers pre-dating the last glaciation, reflected reindeer and woolly rhino being dominant and evidence of human

---

[3] Ibid, p. 2
[4] Ibid, p. 6

2.2 – Excavations at Pin Hole cave during the 1920s
(© Creswell Heritage Trust)

occupation being very rare – only a few crude implements of quartzite were noted. The very bottom Lower Palaeolithic zone (although Middle Palaeolithic in date) of Pin Hole cave, approximately 9-12 feet below the modern (1920s) cave floor harboured roughly chipped hand-axes of Acheulean type and two implements made from mammoth tusk. This is confusing as the layer clearly relates to a Neanderthal use, whilst the mammoth tusk implements are more likely Upper Palaeolithic – evidence for Neanderthals using this material only occurs in the Neanderthal to Modern Human transitional stage, and even then is very rare, and probably not at Creswell Crags. Armstrong's final opinion from the first season at Pin Hole was that it was most probably occupied casually rather than continuously.

Also in 1924, between April and October, Armstrong undertook excavations at Mother Grundy's Parlour, concentrating on the rock shelter at the forefront of the cave. Initial examination in May 1923 of the section created by past excavation revealed 'flint flakes and other evidence'[5] that suggested the cave platform had not been previously investigated. Trial holes confirmed this and on the western side evidence of a living and workshop site were noted. The continuous need to empty and re-fill the excavation area due to its close location to the road meant that progress was slow and only 100sq feet were excavated, although five distinct layers were revealed that matched Boyd Dawkins' stratigraphy from Chamber A.

5 – existing surface layer of cave earth and 'spoil' from past excavations. Teeth of bison and hyaena mixed in with remains of coal fires and clay pipes confirmed this.

4 – old surface layer of a dark, sandy humus material approximately 6 inches thick containing charcoal, ashes, Medieval, Romano-British and 'Late Celtic' (presumably Iron Age) pottery and a few flints.

---

[5] A L Armstrong *Excavations at Mother Grundy's Parlour*, Journal of the Royal Anthropological Institute, Vol. 55, 1924, p. 148

3 – a red cave earth, 2-3ft thick and in places discoloured by fire. Finds included: engraved bones, flint and bone implements, quartzite pebble pot boilers, split bone fragments (of which many showed signs of fire), animal bones and teeth. The layer's composition (it contained an assortment of rocks and debris most likely from the cliff above) and inclusions suggests a slow accumulation over a period that witnessed 'an entire change in climatic conditions and in fauna'.[6] No well defined evidence of occupation was discovered except at the very top and bottom of the layer. At the bottom flints and fractured bones were numerous and suggested an 'almost continuous occupation during the deposition of that portion'[7] (the first 12 inches of make-up above layer 2). The next 9 inches reflect a more casual occupation before the final top 6 inches again bears evidence of a more prolonged habitation.

2 – a yellow cave earth, similar to that in the Pin Hole cave and suggested by Armstrong to be of Lower Mousterian date,[8] contained a few flint flakes with only slight signs of use. Armstrong believed this to suggest the items were dropped and accidentally trodden into the subsoil.[9] Finds of quartzite implements and bones of lion, reindeer, hyaena, woolly rhino and mammoth support a Neanderthal date.

1 – a yellow sand, determined to be a basement layer and housing no fossils or finds.

Within the yellow cave earth (2) a hearth was discovered, scooped out of the cave floor to approximately 9 inches in depth and lined with limestone fragments. It was full of ashes, a piece of mammoth ivory, fragments of split and charred bone and flint flakes. Surrounding the hearth were bone splinters, split bones (for the extraction of marrow as evidenced by the 'marrow scoop' found in the same area), flints, bone tools and the pieces of engraved bone discussed shortly.

Of the bone objects discovered, it is worth noting the piece of cylindrical rod (possibly the shaft of a bone point) made from reindeer antler and polished smooth, the bevel end of a single bevel lance point and a couple of bone awls and other such tools. Relating to the engraved examples of bone, Armstrong mentions that around 500 pieces of bone were systematically washed, dried and examined and that three of these were found to be engraved. One allegedly depicts a reindeer, another a bison (of which Armstrong believed that further cuts and engraved lines may suggest that it was once part of a larger, decorated bone object) and the final example is the head and horns of a rhino, which would have been quite important if true as only six other depictions of rhino are known within the

2.3 – Bone 'marrow scoop' from Mother Grundy's Parlour (M. Beresford, redrawn from Armstrong, 1924)

---

[6] Ibid, p. 150
[7] Ibid, p. 150
[8] Ibid, p. 149
[9] Ibid, p. 149

2.4 – *Bone 'engravings' from Mother Grundy's Parlour. Bison (left), Reindeer (middle), Rhinocerous (right)*
(M. Beresford, redrawn from Armstrong, 1924)

Palaeolithic world.[10] All three bone 'engravings' are contemporary with the hearth, and the reindeer example may even show slight signs of burning.[11] These were the initial interpretations made by Armstrong. However, the portable art 'engravings' were not without their doubters, markedly similar to that of the horse found in Robin Hood Cave by Mello. Generally, of the three, only the reindeer example is accepted and this is often grudgingly. Part of the purposed 'rhino' engraving may also be genuine as it is agreed the horn part may well be man-made but the muzzle section is most likely natural markings. With the initial photographs of the engravings[12] subject to the addition of Chinese white to enhance the outline, it may have influenced initial judgement. In the journal *Nature*[13] we hear how Boyd Dawkins dismissed the engravings as the result of root action, Sollas[14] (whilst dismissing Boyd Dawkins claims from the earlier excavations we might remember) sided with Armstrong and supported the engravings, whilst Dorothy Garrod was caught somewhere in the middle, accepting the reindeer and parts of the purposed rhino but dismissing the bison, again as root action.[15] Recently however Bahn[16] has offered that Armstrong may have gotten a little carried away with his interpretations, and was perhaps prone to an 'overactive imagination' rather than purposefully faking the finds, and that current research by Pettitt and Jacobi on the spoil heaps outside the Church Hole, Pin Hole and Robin Hood Caves may well yet conclude these arguments by revealing further portable art engravings. They may, on the other hand, reveal nothing, perhaps silencing the debate on these early contentious finds.

Returning to the stratigraphy of Mother Grundy's Parlour cave, and although Armstrong initially divided this by geology he also felt it necessary to divide it by chronology. This he split into four sections:

> 1 – Base Zone (comprising of the yellow cave earth layer and the base of the red sandy cave earth). The base of this he dated to Neanderthal times, and the upper portion of the yellow cave earth to most likely Aurignacian – this then gives a date to the hearth and the bone engravings, ie. Early Upper Palaeolithic. If the engravings are

---

[10] Ibid, p. 154
[11] Ibid, p. 154
[12] plate XXII in Armstrong's 1924 report, J.R.A.I
[13] see *Nature*, 115/2896, May 1925, pp.658-9
[14] W J Sollas *Ancient Hunters and their Modern Representatives*, New York, 1924
[15] Dorothy Garrod *The Upper Palaeolithic Age in Britain*, Oxford, 1926
[16] Paul G Bahn *Historical Background to the Discovery of Cave Art at Creswell Crags*, in Pettitt, Bahn & Ripoll *Palaeolithic Cave Art at Creswell Crags in European Context*, Oxford, 2007, pp. 1-14

genuine, this would make them very early indeed within European portable art.

2 – Lower Middle Zone (red sandy cave earth). Flints were numerous in this section, along with 2 pieces of mammoth ivory, a reindeer bone implement which had been rubbed down to a sharp edge at one end, showed signs of considerable use and may have been used for skinning,[17] and also the 'marrow scoops'.

3 – Middle Zone (red sandy cave earth). Flints were less abundant but freely distributed. Only one fragment of reindeer, in the form of antler. Horse bones, however, were found in abundance. Again evidence for fire but no hearths and a single bone tool (from horse) was the only bone tool discovered.

4 – Upper Middle Zone (red sandy cave earth). Flints were present along with shells, particularly *helis memoralis*, which was very abundant.

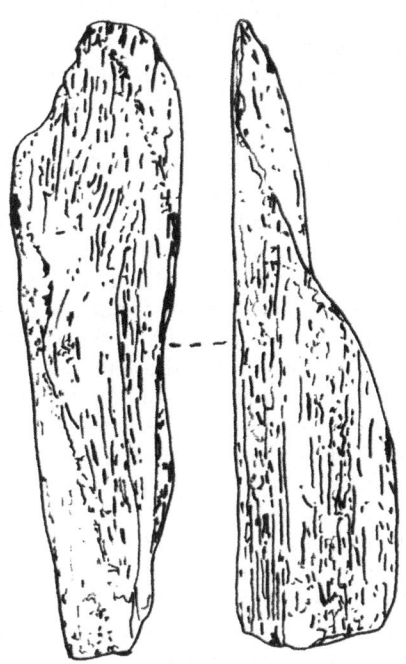

2.5 – *Possible skinning tool from Mother Grundy's Parlour* (M. Beresford, redrawn from Armstrong, 1924)

Finally, considering the flint evidence from Mother Grundy's Parlour, in all 1557 flints were discovered, all of which were obviously imported as flint is not a local resource. One of the most important points to note from Armstrong's report is that he suggests all the flints are somewhat smaller in size than 'Continental prototypes' and there is an 'almost entire absence of cores'.[18] The grey and black cherts native to Derbyshire are entirely absent except for ten pieces found in the upper middle zone. Armstrong points out that this material was used frequently in the 'Transitional industries of the South Yorkshire Moors and the Pennines'[19] (ie. the Palaeolithic – Mesolithic transitory period from circa 8000BC). Generally Mother Grundy's Parlour flints are grey or black in colour and are sourceable to the small nodules with a thin, brown crust that Armstrong suggests may have held their origins within glacial drifts to the South or East (ie. Norfolk or the Lincolnshire Wolds respectively). That some flints bear signs of water-scouring seems to support this. He concludes that the Creswell 'industry as a whole is a rich one and includes most of the typical Upper Palaeolithic forms'[20] such as blades with retouched backs, shouldered points (from the base and lower middle zones) resembling the Solutréan *point-à-cran* (of the Upper Aurignacian and associated with Chatelperronian and Gravette points), 'modified' versions of

---

[17] Armstrong *Excavations at Mother Grundy's Parlour*, p. 154
[18] Ibid, p. 155
[19] Ibid, p. 156
[20] Ibid, p. 156

shouldered points (in the middle and upper middle zones) that are quite geometric in form and finally transitional types (so into the Mesolithic) such as the Azilian and early Tardenoisian microliths in the very final layers of Mother Grundy's Parlour.

In summary Armstrong came to the conclusion that the faunal remains, bone and flint artefacts suggest a periodic occupation, perhaps by hunting parties over an extensive period. The base and upper middle zones were contemporary with a fauna of rhino, mammoth, hyaena, lion and reindeer with a periodic occupation up until more genial climatic conditions where horse and bison were dominant and a more continuous habitation became apparent, perhaps as a camping ground, up to the Azilio-Tardenoisian culture (Mesolithic). The yellow cave earth (2) of Mother Grundy's Parlour could be seen as being contemporary with the red upper cave earth of Pin Hole suggesting the two were occupied at the same time, a period when a developing 'Creswell culture' became apparent. Armstrong argued that the discovery of the engraved double bevel lance point from Pin Hole was of Magdalenian design and 'not merely a survival'[21] and that a shouldered point flint and ivory point shared direct parallels with examples from the cave at La Madeleine, France itself. This, he argued, gave a contemporary date for the corresponding levels at La Madeleine and at Pin Hole, and that further shouldered points from Mother Grundy's Parlour tied in this 'Creswell culture' with the Continental Magdalenian. Apart from at Kent's Cavern, in southern Britain, the Magdalenian culture had at this point little in the way of evidence in British sites but now had unmistakable evidence at Creswell, of that much Armstrong was sure.

He backed up his theory of a definite 'Creswell culture' as opposed to a more general European Magdalenian at Creswell by stating that 'it is scarcely reasonable to expect in any one period of time a close similarity in type of implements and technique, between English and Continental sites of contemporary date. Close parallels are not found to-day in the ordinary implements of life, agriculture, etc, even in adjacent countries, or in colonies of British people abroad, despite commercial enterprise and mechanical production. Therefore, why look for close parallels in Palaeolithic times?'[22] The opinion was that the 'Creswell culture' was traditionally Aurignacian but had Solutréan and Magdalenian influence most probably from passing hunting parties. This suggests a gradual development of flint implements and evidence from Mother Grundy's Parlour appeared to support this, with Armstrong concluding that 'the Mother Grundy's Parlour site is Magdalenian *in age*, Aurignacian *in technique* (both author's emphasis) and that it demonstrates a development of Upper Palaeolithic culture in England, possibly a local development... which may, as further evidence accumulates, prove to be typical of the country as a whole'.[23]

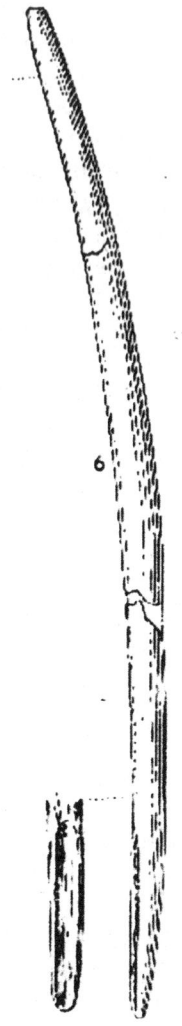

2.6 – Bone reindeer point from Church Hole cave (Garrod, 1926)

---

[21] Ibid, p. 172-3
[22] Ibid, p. 174
[23] Ibid, p. 174

This belief was shared by the pioneering archaeologist Dorothy Garrod who discussed at length the idea of a 'Creswell culture' in her work *The Upper Palaeolithic Age in Britain* published in 1926 just after Armstrong had finished his initial excavations at Creswell. We shall consider Garrod's work in due course, but must first turn our attention to the report filed by J Wilfrid Jackson of Manchester Museum on the faunal remains from Mother Grundy's Parlour.[24] In this report, he notes some interesting points, principally that the reindeer antlers found in the early excavations at Creswell are indicative of the smaller Barren-ground type reindeer rather than the woodland variety and that regarding the red deer, which had been noted by Boyd Dawkins previously in surface soils and disturbed red sandy cave earth of Mother Grundy's Parlour, Robin Hood Cave and Church Hole caves respectively, the remains discovered by Armstrong at Mother Grundy's Parlour now proved conclusively its existence at Creswell within the Pleistocene. Concerning horses, examination of a tooth found at Mother Grundy's Parlour indicated a 'forest' or Solutré breed for the Creswell area. Finally, and perhaps most interestingly, amongst the faunal remains a human upper canine was noted. Previously, the discovery of the skull in Mother Grundy's Parlour had been attributed to the Neolithic or perhaps even later but now, believed Jackson, this interpretation may need re-thinking and the skull could actually be of Aurignacian date. If this was the case, the implications would have been remarkable. Unfortunately, it was to prove a false hope, as we shall see later.

Garrod's opinion on the skull was that it 'appeared undisturbed'[25] whilst Armstrong thought a re-examination would be desirable.[26] She also shared Armstrong's opinion on the chronology of Mother Grundy's Parlour, particularly regarding the faunal remains examined by Jackson – 'it will be seen that the difference in fauna between the Base and Upper Middle is well marked, but that the change is quite gradual, the disappearance of the mammoth and reindeer and the arrival of the red deer occurring between the Lower Middle and Middle Zones'.[27] Garrod's support of Armstrong's work is clear, describing the Pin Hole excavations as being of 'first-rate importance' in highlighting the 'Creswell industry' and suggesting that the double-bevelled ivory javelin head was engraved with a decorative motif 'well-known in Magdalenian levels',[28] thus reinforcing Armstrong's correlations between the so-called 'Creswell industry' and the wider Magdalenian.

This 'Creswell industry', termed the 'Creswellian' by Garrod, could be further evidenced by noting obvious correlations between some of the flints from Robin Hood Cave and Mother Grundy's Parlour at Creswell and also at Aveline's Hole to the south; they were small, angular and with inverse retouch and 'must therefore correspond in time with some phase of the Magdalenian'.[29] Mello's incised horse, also, corresponds with these flints and is again of Magdalenian 'spirit and technique' Garrod argued. She even reinterpreted some of the earlier finds, such as the notched bone 'pendant' found at Church Hole by Boyd Dawkins, as being of a similar typology: '(the) use of tabular bone and the crenellation of the edge'[30] suggested a Middle Magdalenian rather than a Middle Aurignacian date, as initially suggested by Boyd Dawkins.

Equally scathing was Garrod on the issue (brought up once again) of the Machairodus tooth: 'a tooth of Machairodus Latidens was found in the cave-earth (of Robin Hood

---

[24] J Wilfrid Jackson *Report on the animal remains found at the cave known as Mother Grundy's Parlour, Creswell*, in Armstrong *Excavations at Mother Grundy's Parlour*, Journal of the Royal Anthropological Institute, Vol. 55, 1924, pp. 176-78
[25] Garrod *Upper Palaeolithic*, p. 136
[26] Ibid, p. 136
[27] Ibid, p. 139-41
[28] Ibid, p. 147
[29] Ibid, p. 148
[30] Ibid, p. 149

30 Beyond the Ice

2.7 – Replica of an engraved bone object of Magdalenian design from Creswell Crags (M. Beresford)

Cave) by one of the workmen, but some doubt has been thrown on the genuineness of this discovery. In any case the tooth can hardly have been contemporary with the rest of the bones'.[31] Also from Robin Hood Cave Garrod discusses the fragment of an awl or stiletto made from reindeer bone that she interprets as being of Upper Aurignacian date and bears similarities to an example found on the Continent at Wildscheuer, Nassau.[32]

Regarding the Church Hole cave, Garrod discusses the stone tool evidence and suggests that 'the quartzite implements from the red sand and the base of the cave-earth are of the same type as those found in Robin Hood's Cave and therefore probably Mousterian. The flint industry is of Upper Palaeolithic type, but very scanty'.[33] Scanty indeed. Boyd Dawkins stressed that of the 70-80 flint flakes found in the Church Hole only 8 were definite implements.[34] We can tell from the quartzite and the relevant fauna that the early layers are of Neanderthal date and the suggestion that at least two of the flints are of La Gravette type suggest an Early Upper Palaeolithic date. That some of the bone artefacts are of reindeer might suggest a similar date, and yet the horse bone pendant is interesting as it suggests a later date (given the fauna of the bone) and that it shares similarities with the Magdalenian seems to support this. So there appears a varied habitation or use of Church Hole but nowhere near on the same scale as the other caves. Perhaps the reason for this lies in the discovery of the cave art in 2003, which shall be discussed in detail in the next chapter.

The following year, after Garrod's seminal work was published, Armstrong began his second season of excavations in Pin Hole. In 1927 the excavation of the passageway was completed and work began on the entrance to the chamber. Here he found the skull of a cave bear, the rather rare remains of a duck egg and quite interestingly the fish bones of pike and lemon sole, which would suggest some link with the sea.[35] The inner chamber was excavated between 1928-29 and in Armstrong's opinion the results strengthened the conclusions he came to after the 1924-26 season. One important, and once again controversial, discovery was that of the engraving of a human figure incised on the rib

---

[31] Ibid, p. 124
[32] Ibid, p. 129
[33] Ibid, p. 133
[34] Ibid, p. 133
[35] Armstrong *Excavations at Creswell Crags, Pin Hole Cave, 1925-28*, in *Transactions of the Hunter Archaeological Society*, 1929, Vol. III, p.332

bone of a rhinoceros, discovered on Easter Sunday 1928 in the south-east corner of the chamber and described as 'the most important object so far found at Creswell'.[36]

The anthropomorphic engraving (that is half man, half animal) was suggested by Armstrong to be a 'masked human figure in the act of dancing a ceremonial dance'[37] a quite bold statement given the engraving's crude form. He described it as being drawn with a 'fine incised line, in profile, representing the right hand side, but the feet are not shown. The right leg is slightly bent, the left raised and bent at the knee, the genitalia being accentuated. The right arm is extended, and a club, or bow, is held in the hand. A line across the body at the waist may represent a belt, the bottom edge of the mask or possibly is part of the object held in the hand. The head is covered with an animal mask, giving an ape-like appearance to the figure'.[37] Armstrong believed that the Creswell example was quite similar to examples from the Continent such as those from Altamira (Spain) and Chancelade (France), again reflecting a wider European context.

In the local press this point was further stressed; the *Sheffield Telegraph* of 7th January 1925 featuring an article headed 'Creswell Caves: Haunts of Prehistoric Man' in which it informed us of how 'influential' *cultures* rather than *peoples* from the Continent affected our own past – '(the) Magdalenian marks a similar incursion which profoundly affected Central France...whether or not this extended to Britain has of late been disputed. Certainly its influence did, but that (its) people did has yet to be established'.[38] The article further

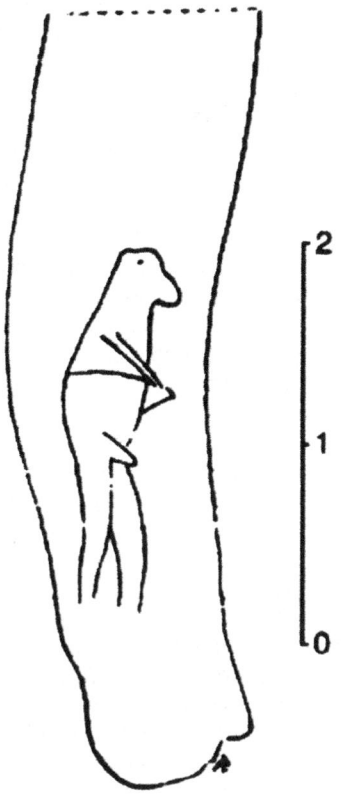

2.8 – *The anthropomorphic engraving from Pin Hole cave (Armstrong, 1929)*

attempted to explain the various terminology linked with Creswell to the 'general reader', terms such as Aurignacian and Tardenoisian, suggesting they could well become widely recognised terms alongside more easily understood labels as Norman or Jacobean. It is fair to say, some 80 years on, the majority of 'general readers' would still find these Prehistoric cultures rather obscure within the historical spectrum. How far we have moved on since this statement was written in the press in the 1920s is reflected by yet another paragraph from the article that suggests how 'everyone knows' that there are two periods of the Stone Age: the Palaeolithic (Old Stone Age) and the Neolithic (New Stone Age), but today we widely recognise the Mesolithic (Middle Stone Age) separating these periods and reflecting just that Azilio-Tardenoisian culture referred to. In the wider press, *The Times* of 22nd December 1924 also downplayed a definite link between Creswell and Europe: 'the implements (at Creswell) clearly show that the

---

[36] Armstrong *Discovery of an Engraved Drawing of a Masked Human Figure*, in *Proceedings of the Prehistoric Society,* 1929, Vol. VI, p. 29
[37] Ibid, p. 29
[38] *Creswell Caves: Haunts of Prehistoric Man, Sheffield Telegraph,*7th January 1925

culture developed there independently from late Aurignacian to Azilio-Tardenoisian times, free from any Magdalenian influence'.[39]

Armstrong's final period of excavations at Pin Hole came to confirm this view, in his opinion, but also brought further information relating to Creswell's past to light. Between 1931-32 the passage was excavated some 25ft from the main chamber and to a thickness of up to 3m in places. This deposit was deemed to be Middle Mousterian in date as it contained a number of quartzite tools, flint and bone implements and four small perforated phalanges – 'apparently amulets'.[40] These would be quite rare, if amulets, as artefacts of this kind had never before been found in Mousterian deposits. The conclusions from these excavations confirmed that the cave reflected no disturbance by glacial inflow and as a result the cave's archaeology was a 'record of Creswell's past and covers the whole period of the last major glaciation in England. The lowest level, Mousterian 1, had a principally quartzite industry with a fauna of horse, bison and giant deer (a warm fauna). Overlying this was a 'slab layer' of massive slabs and rocks, which reflected a dramatic drop in temperature. It was void of human evidence but the fauna was of arctic type.[41]

Mousterian 2 reflected a gradual warming period once more, with horse, bison and giant deer returning. Again, however, a renewed cold period is evidenced with an arctic fauna, scant human traces and once again massive stone slabs being encountered. One of the most interesting finds from this level, found in August 1934, was that of a suggested 'bull-roarer' – *'at one end, the thickest portion of the bone, a hole for suspension has been drilled by the rotation of a pointed tool. This is of "hour-glass" section, indicating drilling from both sides, and the hole is placed slightly out of the centre line of the object. The material is part of the long bone of a large animal, probably bison or mammoth, and in section is slightly convex on one surface (the natural outer surface of the bone) and flat upon the other. The flat surface bears evidence of having been originally rubbed down and polished by friction upon a fine-grained sandstone, and the edges have received similar treatment in order to produce the symmetrical outline.'*[42] Study of the artefact by various specialists deemed it to be a bull-roarer of 'typical form' and 'in view of the object's resemblance to a bull-roarer, a string was attached, and, when whirled rapidly, it proved to give out the characteristic note of such.'[43] It was found along with the aforementioned phalanges as well as bone piercers and other worked-bone tools, leading Armstrong to suggest that they may indicate 'a higher degree of culture than has generally been assigned to Mousterian man'.[44] Once again it seems that Armstrong either got his dating wrong or the deposits had been mixed (by glacial waters for example) as bone tools such as these are Late Palaeolithic, ie. from Modern Humans.

Mousterian 3 was the upper limit of the lower cave-earth and again harboured an arctic fauna. Its layers merged into the proto-Solutréan and Aurignacian levels of the upper cave-earth. Armstrong pointed out that the fluctuations in the climate, evident in the Pin Hole geology, corresponded with Penck and Brückner's glacial epoch episodes, that is the Würm 1, the Laufern retreat, and Würm 2. This theory is certainly supported by the geology within the cave, not least the colour difference between the cave-earths, but most strikingly in the lower cave-earth rocks and fragments of limestone were extremely

---

[39] *Palaeolithic Man in England: New Light on Age of Cavemen, The Times,* 22nd December 1924
[40] Armstrong *Excavations at Creswell Crags, Derbyshire 1928-32: The Pin Hole Cave, Transactions of the Hunter Archaeological Society,* 1937, Vol. IV, p. 178
[41] Ibid, p. 179
[42] Armstrong *A Bull-roarer of Le Moustier age from Pin Hole Cave, Creswell Crags, Derbyshire, Antiquaries Journal,* 16, 1939, p. 322
[43] Ibid, p. 323
[44] Ibid, p. 323

CORRELATION.	CLIMATE.	SECTION.		CULTURE.
LATE PLEISTOCENE BOULDER CLAYS OF YORKS LINCS NORFOLK AND NORTH WALES.	GLACIAL			STALAGMITE.
	WET & COLD.		UPPER CAVE-EARTH	DEVELOPED AURIGNACIAN. (MAGDALENIAN AGE)
INTER GLACIAL.	TEMPERATE.	RED CAVE-EARTH.		FONT ROBERT LEVEL. UPPER AURIGNACIAN & PROTO SOLUTREAN.
	COLD			MOUSTERIAN 3.
WÜRM 2.	GLACIAL			SLAB LAYER (2)
INTERGLACIAL. (LAUFEN RETREAT.)	COLD. MODERATELY WARM. COLD	YELLOW CAVE-EARTH.	EARTH	MOUSTERIAN 2.
WÜRM 1.	GLACIAL.			SLAB LAYER (1)
	COLD.		LOWER CAVE	
RISS - WÜRM INTER GLACIAL.	MODERATELY WARM.	YELLOW CAVE - EARTH		MOUSTERIAN 1
		BED ROCK		STERILE.

2.9 – *Typical section of the Pin Hole Cave*
(Armstrong, 1937)

decomposed and had often been reduced to dolomitic sand. The upper cave-earth simply did not contain this evidence and its fragments were hard and unchanged. In his 1937 report, Armstrong mentioned how Professor Fearnsides of Sheffield University believed that this difference was caused by 'the chemical action of comparatively still water upon the Magnesium Limestone during a prolonged period of immersion (in water)'[45] ie. the cave was waterlogged. Further work on samples of both cave-earths (again at Sheffield University) confirmed this theory, but also suggested that initially both cave-earths had the *same* geological composition and had not at any point been introduced 'by running water' (that is, glacial inflow).

In the 1920s and 30s the entrance to Pin Hole was some 31ft above the stream within the gorge. Armstrong argued that a barrier, perhaps comprised of rocks or boulder-clay, existed at the eastern end of the gorge and that the huge increase of water from melting ice caused an 'extensive basin' to the west of it (around Boat House Cave and Mother Grundy's Parlour) which inevitably created a large lake which, in turn, caused extensive erosion and hollowing back of the crag faces. He further argued that studies of the gorge supported this, as does traceable evidence of his theory within the gorge as well, and that the notable horizontal plane of this erosion ties in accordingly with the decomposition evidence noted on the walls of Pin Hole (and tying in with the geological differences of the two cave-earths). The fauna of the upper cave-earth suggests a fluctuation in temperature, perhaps hot summers with rather cold winters but a more harsh and cold climate at the bottom of the layer and at the top also. The presence of reindeer throughout supports this.

That stalagmitic formation is void from both cave-earths but 'crowns' the top of the upper and the cave walls and may suggest a prolonged period of heavy rainfall, causing the cave to become unfit for either human or animal occupation – the upper two thirds of the stalagmite is void of relics.[46] It also appears to have been the factor that 'finally drove out the Pleistocene fauna,'[47] the layer above reflected only brown bear, wolf, red deer, badger and pig. Armstrong believed that 'climatic conditions of great severity' would have been necessary and it may be that a 'minor glaciation' can be correlated with the Late Glacial Hessle Clay of Yorkshire and Lincolnshire and the Brown Boulder Clay of Norfolk. We may note that in the 'final Pleistocene glaciation' at Creswell, man may have been driven out of Pin Hole but instead occupied Mother Grundy's Parlour, which Armstrong's work suggests.

Amongst the many bones collected within the Armstrong excavations at Pin Hole were a number of fragmentary human remains, although these were not noted at the time. According to Jenkinson[48] they were reportedly first recognised by Kitching[49] as human remains, but in a letter[50] between Don Brothwell and Dr. Owen of University Museum, Manchester dated 14th February 1962, Brothwell clearly states that he had made some notes on the bone remains 'a few months earlier' (so presumably towards the end of 1961). Brothwell describes them thus:

> **LL 1627** – left temporal of an immature individual. Its general size is not quite as large as in the adult English skull, whether male or female. The mastoid process is small

---

[45] Armstrong *Excavations at Creswell,* 1937, p. 181
[46] Ibid, p. 183
[47] Ibid, p. 183
[48] Jenkinson *Creswell Crags: Late Pleistocene Sites in the East Midlands,* (Oxford) 1984
[49] Kitching *Bone, tooth and Horn Tools of Palaeolithic Man: an Account of the Osteodontokeratic Discoveries in the Pin Hole Cave, Derbyshire,* (Manchester) 1963
[50] The letter is part of a larger collection referenced as the *Armstrong Manuscripts* within the archives at both Sheffield Museum and Creswell Crags

but no more so than is normal for young individuals. Considering overall size and general development of the mastoid process, etc, the person was probably no more than fifteen years of age.

LL 1626 – nearly complete ilium belonging to a juvenile, again approximately 15 years of age.

LL 1629 – most of a clavicle of an adult individual...size and rugedness suggests a male.

LL 1628 – small fragment of an immature skull.

Jenkinson states that six pieces were found (although Brothwell mentions only four in his notes) and that the remains belong to at least four individuals, two adults and two juveniles. He further believes that the way in which the remains were fragmented are 'difficult to explain away as natural or post-mortem fractures'[51] and that Late Palaeolithic sites often reflect human remains fractured in this way. So, if the remains are of a Late Palaeolithic date, and the stratigraphy seems to confirm that they are (they were found within stratigraphic layers 2, 3 and 4), then they may indicate 'ritual activity involving human corpses during the Upper Palaeolithic.[52] This subject shall be dealt with further in chapter 5.

Armstrong's work has proven extremely important in shaping how we view Creswell's past and went above and beyond what the earlier antiquarian investigations revealed. Yet, much like these antiquarian results, time would once again test the interpretations suggested. Re-examination of the findings and further excavations and analysis of the caves in the subsequent years again raised questions on the earlier interpretations, not least challenging the idea of an exclusive localised industry in the Creswellian and the influence that the wider European Magdalenian culture had on Creswell. Before we focus on this recent work, we must first turn our attention to what will probably always be known as Creswell's finest hour, the discovery of the cave art in 2003, an occasion that arguably finally put Creswell, and Britain, firmly on the Palaeolithic map.

---

[51] Jenkinson, *Creswell Crags*, p. 81
[52] Ibid, p. 81

3
Discovery of the Rock Art at Church Hole Cave, Creswell Crags and its Wider Implications

> *'The discovery of the art, and the clear parallels between it and contemporary Magdalenian art on the continent, form a strong indication of the integral connection between the hunter-gatherers operating in and around Creswell and those far to the south and east'*
>
> Paul Pettitt, *Current Archaeology Magazine,* (May/June, 2005)

When Ice Age cave art was discovered at Creswell Crags in April 2003 it caused international excitement and attention from all walks of life. The lack of authentic discoveries in the past in Britain had led to the general consensus that cave art was unique to our continental cousins, chiefly France, Spain and Italy. But, just as Paul Bahn had argued in the previous chapter with regards genuine portable art, just because it had yet to be discovered did not necessarily mean it did not exist. Debatable or not, we now have portable art from British Ice Age sites, so why not parietal art? Belgium also shares this apparent theme: it has rich evidence of occupied caves and portable art, but again no parietal art. Fortunately for us, Bahn was not to be dissuaded: 'since portable art of the period had long been known in this country, it had always seemed probable that parietal art must also have existed'.[1]

Earlier claims made by the abbè Henri Breuil and W J Sollas in 1912 of ten painted red lines at the cave of Bacon Hole, Somerset turned out to be at best extremely questionable, especially as they failed to authenticate the alleged art. The matter resolved itself when the lines eventually faded, much to the discoverers' embarrassment and the general belief is that they may have been created by a Victorian sailor simply cleaning his brush

---

[1] Paul G. Bahn *The Historical Background to the Discovery of Cave Art at Creswell Crags,* in Pettitt, Bahn & Rippoll *Palaeolithic Cave Art at Creswell Crags in European Context,* (Oxford) 2007, p. 1

on the cave wall.[2] There were further false claims[3] that undoubtedly aided the degree of apprehension about the likelihood of British cave art, and yet it always remained the ultimate dream of Paul Bahn to one day discover the first British Ice Age art: '(I had) wanted to find Ice Age cave art in Britain for more than 25 years, and that dream has finally come true'.[4]

It was whilst attending a formal dinner at Keble College, Oxford that Bahn discussed his wish to one-day search for cave art in Britain with Paul Pettitt (the two had just written an article together for *Antiquity* on the cave art at Chauvet). Instantly, Pettitt expressed his interest in the project and the pair enlisted the Spanish cave art expert Sergio Rippoll (whom Bahn describes as having the 'keenest eyes I know, as well as a lot of luck, which is equally important')[5] with a date of Easter 2003 pencilled in. As Paul Bahn was based in Hull at the time the trio began their search at Creswell Crags, the nearest site geographically, and the rest, as they say, is history – quite literally! On first inspection of the Creswell caves, and particularly in Church Hole, there is an obvious element of graffiti dating back into at least the 19th century – a certain J. Gascoyne inscribed the phrase 'And such is the Kingdom of God' dated to April 12th 1870 whilst a 'PM' carved his initials with a date of 1948.[6]

The survey at Creswell was part of a wider nationwide sweep of known Late Upper Palaeolithic (Creswellian) cave sites, the period the team deemed most likely to harbour cave art. However, as Paul Pettitt explains 'although we undertook an initial survey of several caves across the British south and Midlands, we found art only at Creswell Crags'.[7] The four major caves at Creswell (Church Hole, Robin Hood Cave, Pin Hole, Mother Grundy's Parlour) were surveyed on 14th April 2003 and art was noted in all but Pin Hole – a couple of triangular 'vulvae' symbols in Robin Hood Cave, a boomerang or banana shaped engraving (possibly an animal head) in Mother Grundy's Parlour and a series of engravings in Church Hole.

The most likely reason why the art had previously remained undetected in Church Hole was because the 19th century excavations had emptied the cave of its soil, meaning the current floor level is considerably lower than in the Late Upper Palaeolithic, to which the art was believed to date. This meant that it was high above eye level, and only the keen eye of Sergio Rippoll noticing a suspicious looking engraved line towards the cave ceiling stopped the cave art from being missed once again. Upon inspection, with the aid of a rather narrow overhang platform protruding from the cave wall, Sergio realised he was looking into the face of what he believed to be an Ice Age engraving of an ibex.

Rippoll[8] explains how they undertook a systematic study from the cave entrance, along the left wall to the far end of the cave and then back along the right hand wall. They identified twelve decorated surfaces (panels), five on the left wall and seven on the right.

---

[2] from *The Times*, October 14th, 1912
[3] the *Illustrated London News* ran a story in 1981 claiming the discovery of cave engravings at Symonds Yat in the Wye Valley, but upon investigation the 'engravings' turned out to be completely natural markings
[4] Paul Bahn speaking in *Art of the Hunters, British Archaeology*, September 2003, pp.9-13
[5] Ibid.
[6] personal observation. The phrase is from Mark 10:14.
[7] Paul Pettitt *Palaeolithic cave art found in Britain*, in *Before Farming*, 2003/3 (10)
[8] Sergio Rippoll & Francisco Muñoz *The Palaeolithic Rock Art of Creswell Crags: Prelude to a Systematic Study* in Pettitt et al *Palaeolithic Cave Art*, p. 14-15

38 BEYOND THE ICE

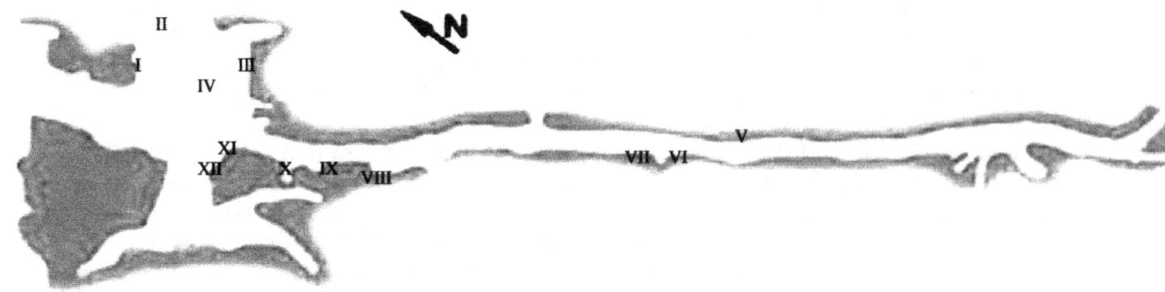

3.1 – *Plan of Church Hole cave depicting the twelve 'panels' of Ice Age art*
(M. Beresford)

Left-hand wall

Panel I: head of bovid, possibly an auroch
Panel II: symbol, oval with a curved base. To the right is a series of unconnected lines
Panel III: stag, incomplete depiction of a quadruped (possibly a young stag) and a bison
Panel IV: bird (bas-relief), proposed bison (possibly natural) and a headless horse
Panel V: triangle (possibly a vulva)

Right-hand wall

Panel VI: two incised lines (one vertical, one horizontal)
Panel VII: controversial 'bird' panel
SR / PB view – on the left possibly a crane (lower image) while the bigger outline (in the middle) remains under study. The three images on the right are geese of differing sizes
PP view – female figures (discussed in detail later)
Panel VIII: series of linear grooves which in one case form an angle
Panel IX: series of very superficial, unconnected lines
Panel X: two possible bird depictions
Panel XI: series of unconnected, shallow lines, one of which is curved
Panel XII: two triangle-shaped symbols, possibly vulvae

Robin Hood Cave

Triangular-shaped engraving, probably a vulva, and possibly depicting the start of the hips and waist (right wall, 7.35m from entrance, 3.3m above present floor)

Mother Grundy's Parlour

Small symbol (15cm long by 6cm wide), boomerang shaped, but right-hand part is not closed

On discovering the cave art, Pettitt stressed the implications of the find, telling how 'the discovery dispels the dogma that no cave art would be found in Britain, and opens up a new paradigm in which archaeologists will take the surveying of caves for art very

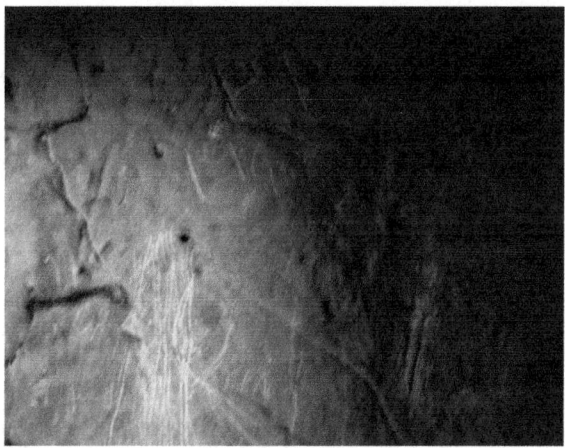

3.2 – *Deer Stag engraving (panel III), showing modern grafitti and 'goatee beard'*
(M. Beresford)

seriously'.[9] Something that strikes as being quite interesting is the comment Paul Bahn made in September 2003 when he looked back on the discovery. Here, he stressed his belief that short of finding a new cave or a new chamber within a known cave, no examples of cave art were likely to come to light, as surely someone would have noticed them previously.[10] But, with the Church Hole engravings (well, at least one of them) someone had! If we look closely at the engraving initially deemed to be an ibex we can see it has quite obviously been given a 'goatee' beard, perhaps by the PM mentioned earlier, whose graffiti from 1948 lies just centimetres away from the 'beard'. Furthermore, during a cave tour into Church Hole after the art was discovered, one visitor claimed that they knew who PM was, and that he was a local man from the village of Creswell who played in the caves as a boy.[11] Rather curiously, Bahn spoke of the graffiti on the ibex thus: 'by some miracle the graffiti – whose creators had doubtless not seen the animal figure – missed the head, which remains pristine'.[12] The 'goatee beard' adornment suggests quite the opposite, that someone with a keen eye had indeed noticed the animal before, and if they had only mentioned their discovery they could have staked their place in Ice Age history.

In June the team returned to Creswell to properly record the artwork, aided by a scaffold platform erected in line with the Late Upper Palaeolithic floor levels funded by English Heritage. This allowed for a better inspection and further images were discovered including the bovid of panel I. In all, ten images had been recognised by July 2003. News of the discovery was then made public, gaining world-wide media attention.

In April the following year, a second season of investigation was carried out, with further discoveries being made. The *Guardian* of Thursday 15th April 2004 told of 'the discovery of 13,000 year old rock paintings in Nottinghamshire (which have) rewrote ice-age history in Britian'.[13] Here we must be careful as the art was in the form of *engravings* and not *paintings* as suggested by the article. Jon Humble, Inspector of Ancient Monuments for English Heritage described it as being 'the best and most successful

---

[9] Pettitt, *Palaeolithic cave art,* 2003
[10] Bahn *Art of the Hunters,* 2003
[11] Anna Griffiths, Creswell Crags Heritage Officer, pers. comm.
[12] Bahn, *Art of the Hunters,* 2003
[13] *Dancing girls and the merry Magdalenian,* The *Guardian*, Thursday 15th April 2004

example of an archaeology-led project for social and economic regeneration anywhere in the UK'.[14] The 2004 season exceeded the previous season in terms of results, as the natural light created by the sunny weather proved far more useful for detecting the art than the artificial lighting used in 2003. Observations by the author noted that using the natural light is by far the best way to view the engravings; shining a torch onto the art can, at times, render it almost invisible (for some of the less obvious pieces) and even water percolating through the rock on particularly wet days can hinder the viewing process.

By the end of the 2004 season, then, around ninety images had been detected, although the British members of the team are a little more reserved on this figure. Of these ninety, fifty-eight are situated on the ceiling and only the 'bird / female' panel and one of the vulva panels are located away from the entrance chamber and within complete darkness. Speaking in *Antiquity* in June 2004, Bahn revealed how 'bas-reliefs on cave ceilings are extremely rare even on the continent... it is obvious that Church Hole possesses the most richly carved and engraved ceiling in the whole of cave art, and this within quite a small surface area'[15] (c.14m^2). The discovery meant that Britain could now be added 'to the distribution map of decorated Ice Age sites in Eurasia'[16] and meant that the most northerly cave art site is now 280 miles further north. With one of the most remarkable finds in British archaeology on their hands, the team set about analysing and interpreting the art and attempted to set it into a wider European context based on form and style.

In September 2003 Paul Bahn, fresh from the newfound discovery, rather excitedly suggested that there is a 'classic phenomenon in archaeology that once something has been looked for, and been shown to exist, it starts to be found elsewhere'.[17] In the case of British cave art, six years later we still await a second discovery, highlighting the importance and uniqueness of the Creswell art. In his paper at *Capra 5*[18] Paul Pettitt admitted that 'to date we have found no convincing evidence of Palaeolithic cave art anywhere else but at Creswell' but reminds us of the possibility of further cave art having been destroyed by the British climate:

> *'it is debatable as to whether or not Britain was more Atlantic in the Pleistocene than, say, southwest France or northern Spain...(it is possible) that increased water flow through caves may on occasion have washed off pigments such as charcoal and ochre (but) it is equally likely to have preserved them under the sheets of calcium carbonate'.*[19]

With regards to the cave art in Britain that most definitely exists, an amount of uncertainty surrounding the purposed ibex began to heighten, particularly problematic as ibex was not known to have existed in Britain in this period. Closer analysis later revealed traces of antlers on the animal's head and we now believe it to be a red deer stag, particularly interesting due to the importance of deer within the Magdalenian world (discussed in detail later). Another area of uncertainty surrounded the suggested 'bird' panel (panel VII) located in the corridor of the cave. Although initially the investigating

---

[14] Ibid.
[15] *New discoveries of Cave Art in Church Hole (Creswell Crags, England)*, Antiquity, Vol. 78, No. 300, June 2004
[16] Bahn, *Art of the Hunters*, 2003
[17] Ibid.
[18] *Discovery, nature and preliminary thoughts about Britain's first cave art*, Pettitt, 2003, Capra 5, available at http://capra.group.shef.ac.uk/5/pettitt.pdf
[19] Ibid.

3.3 – Panel VII at Church Hole: are they birds or stylised females?
(M. Beresford)

team all supported the 'bird' theory for the engravings[20] Paul Pettitt began to have his doubts, and later expressed his theory that they could in fact represent stylised females (discussed at length shortly). To debate these theories, heighten public awareness of the discovery and to involve the local community a special conference was held at the Creswell Social Centre between 15-17 April 2004. The very fact that this conference on the internationally important discovery was held on such a small scale in the locality where the art was discovered is a testament to all involved in the discovery, and is hugely significant in instilling a sense of local pride and interest in not just the art but in the site of Creswell Crags itself.

The 'clear aim of the conference (was) that the importance of the Creswell engravings should not be lost to obscure academic literature'[21] and to 'inform the local people of the finds and show them that they had something of world importance in their midst'.[22] In the *Guardian* on the opening day of the conference, Paul Pettitt was quoted as saying that the Magdalenian period (which the Creswell art almost certainly dated to) was the last time in history that Europe was galvanized into a coherent and unified state, and here appeared to be proof that Britain was part of that 'unified state'.[23]

A year later, in May 2005, Paul Bahn proudly suggested in *Current Archaeology* magazine that 'this small cave (Church Hole) has a total of up to 90 figures, including engravings, bas-relief and paintings. It must have been a splendid sight when pristine'.[24] The painting that Bahn refers to is that of a horse's head depicted on the ceiling of the cave, and whereas its mane is in bas-relief the head itself is neither engraved or pecked but appears to be 'coloured' in a bluish-green substance. Of all the art in the cave, it

---

[20] in the article *Palaeolithic cave art found in Britain,* in *Before Farming,* 2003/3 (10), Pettitt agrees with the 'bird' theory for the art
[21] Claire Fisher & Rob Dinnis *Rewriting the History Books: The Magdalenian Art of Creswell Crags,* in Pettitt et al *Palaeolithic Cave Art,* p.280
[22] *Creswell Crags: Discovering cave art in Britain, Current Archaeology,* No. 197, May / June 2005
[23] *Dancing girls and the merry Magdalenian,* The *Guardian,* Thursday 15th April 2004
[24] *Creswell Crags: Discovering cave art in Britain, Current Archaeology,* No. 197, May / June 2005

is the only one that looks as if it may have once been painted, and sure enough when analysed through infrared photography traces of manganese pigment were identified.[25] Bahn summed up the end of the project and the remarkable results by saying that 'Church Hole is of huge importance not only because of its quantity of figures but also their variety'.[26] With the cave art now out in the public eye and the various theories and suppositions being debated, the team were almost certain that Creswell's art did indeed date to the Creswellian or continental Late Magdalenian period, linking Britain with wider Europe. However, there would always remain an element of doubt, and perhaps due to the false claims of the past, verification of its age was understandably required.

One of the processes used on the Creswell art in order to accurately map, plot and preserve (at least in record form) the engravings was the method of 3D laser scanning, which Alistair Carty explains thus:

> 'the process of recording "in situ" archaeological art can be a time-consuming and complex task...there are considerable challenges to the recorder, including the accurate positioning and fixing of survey frames, the physical discomfort of sitting, crouching or even lying down for long periods of time in cramped surroundings. Furthermore, the more accurate forms of traditional recording include the taking of rubbings of the carvings (which could) increase the potential of damage...3D laser scanning offers solutions to most of these problems by quickly producing a highly dense fully three-dimensional surface map of the art'.[27]

Basically, 3D laser scanning enables us to in effect 'map' the engraved lines within the rock surface – in its simplest form the natural rock face is depicted in a lighter tone, whereas the incised lines are reflected much darker.

This technique has been used to produce high-quality replicas in the past, such as those from the Spanish cave art site of Altamira. It also does this in such a way as to be 'non-contact', something that is highly prioritised in modern archaeology, and means it conforms to certain preservation demands. As Carty explains 'this technique offers a real possibility of satisfying the various demands on conservation management schemes for access to relatively inaccessible Palaeolithic artworks'.[28]

The question with the art, then, remained as to whether it was Magdalenian in date as was suspected. The initial assessment was based upon the following premises:

- The sharp lines and colours of the graffiti from the 19th and 20th centuries were an obvious contrast to the far duller engravings of the art work
- In numerous places flowstone growth had occurred over the art
- The art was located considerably higher than the modern floor levels, suggesting a certain degree of antiquity
- Much of the art had obvious parallels with Magdalenian continental art
- The bovid depicted a species known to have been extinct in Britain by at least the 17th century

Therefore, it was determined that the 'most appropriate period (for the art) is that of the Creswellian...one cannot rule out that the art is older, although given the scarcity of

---
[25] Ibid.
[26] *New discoveries of Cave Art in Church Hole (Creswell Crags, England)*, Antiquity, Vol. 78, No. 300, June 2004
[27] Alistair Carty *3D Laser Scanning at Church Hole, Creswell Crags*, in Pettitt et al *Palaeolithic Cave Art*, p. 46
[28] Ibid. p. 52

Sample name	U (ppm)	$^{234}U/^{238}U$	$^{230}Th/^{234}U$	$^{230}Th/^{232}Th$	Uncorrected Age (ky)	Corrected Age (ky)[a]
Flowstone overlying 'notches', Church Hole						
CHC-2 top	0.6177 ± 0.0013	1.0845 ± 0.0074	0.1214 ± 0.0028	12.4 ± 0.38	14.12 +0.35/-0.35	13.02 +0.42/-0.39
CHC-B	0.4977 ± 0.0008	1.0798 ± 0.0066	0.0485 ± 0.0013	2.702 ± 0.097	5.43 +0.16/-0.16	3.29 +0.38/-0.38
CHC-C1	0.8532 ± 0.0019	1.0700 ± 0.0077	0.0129 ± 0.0003	3.187 ± 0.107	1.42 +0.04/-0.04	0.85 +0.1/-0.1
CHC-C2	0.5168 ± 0.0011	1.0775 ± 0.0087	0.0911 ± 0.0020	2.049 ± 0.061	10.43 +0.24/-0.24	5.4 +0.91/-0.86
CHC-C6	0.5117 ± 0.0011	1.0967 ± 0.0080	0.0844 ± 0.0015	7.535 ± 0.198	9.63 +0.19/-0.19	8.33 +0.28/-0.29
CHC-C7	0.4892 ± 0.0013	1.0800 ± 0.0101	0.0462 ± 0.0011	7.999 ± 0.259	5.17 +0.13/-0.13	4.47 +0.18/-0.17
Flowstone overlying 'birds', Church Hole						
CHC-E1	1.0177 ± 0.0031	1.2805 ± 0.0102	0.1914 ± 0.0037	2.392 ± 0.064	23.03 +0.50/-0.50	14.4 +1.7/-1.6
CHC-E2	1.2202 ± 0.0028	1.2907 ± 0.0091	0.1487 ± 0.0033	2.405 ± 0.073	17.49 +0.43/-0.43	10.9 +1.2/-1.2
CHC-E3	1.6365 ± 0.0054	1.2922 ± 0.0093	0.0614 ± 0.0017	6.858 ± 0.248	6.91 +0.20/-0.20	5.97 +0.25/-0.25
Flowstone overlying 'vulva', Robin Hood's Cave						
RHC-F1	0.6174 ± 0.0015	1.2343 ± 0.0107	0.0846 ± 0.0035	2.151 ± 0.106	9.63 +0.47/-0.42	5.2 +0.83/-0.82
RHC-F2	0.7771 ± 0.0019	1.2565 ± 0.0105	0.0792 ± 0.0074	11.17 ± 1.140	8.99 +0.89/-0.88	8.20 +0.86/-0.88
Errors given at 2σ.						

3.4 – *U-series results from Church Hole and Robin Hood Cave (M. Beresford. Source: Pike et al, 2007)*

Lab Reference (OxA)	Sample description	Radiocarbon years (BP)	Percentile probability calibrated age range distributions at 95.4% level of confidence
Robin Hood's Cave			
OxA-1616	*L. timidus* cut-marked bone	12600 ± 170	15650-13150 cal. BP (95.4%)
OxA-3416	*L. timidus* cut-marked bone	12580 ± 110	15650-14150 cal. BP (95.4%)
OxA-1618	*L. timidus* cut-marked bone	12480 ± 170	15550-14050 cal. BP (95.4%)
OxA-1619	*L. timidus* cut-marked bone	12450 ± 150	15550-14050 cal. BP (95.4%)
OxA-1917	*L. timidus* cut-marked bone	12420 ± 200	15650-14050 cal. BP (94.3%) 13950-13850 cal. BP (1.1%)
OxA-3415	*L. timidus* cut-marked bone	12430 ± 120	15450-14050 cal. BP (95.4%)
OxA-1670	*L. timidus* cut-marked bone	12290 ± 120	15450-14050 cal. BP (92.7%) 13950-13750 cal. BP (2.7%)
Pin Hole			
OxA-3404	*L. timidus* cut-marked bone	12510 ± 110	15550-14150 cal. BP (95.4%)
OxA-1467	*L. timidus* cut-marked bone	12350 ± 120	15450-14050 cal. BP (95.4%)
Church Hole			
OxA-3717	Antler rod 'scooped end'	12020 ± 100	15275-14675 cal. BP (22.0%) 14340-13805 cal. BP (68.8%) 13780-13640 cal. BP (4.6%)
OxA-3718	Antler rod 'scooped end'	12250 ± 90	15425-14675 cal. BP (46.0%) 14425-14060 cal. BP (45.7%) 13935-13840 cal. BP (3.7%)
OxA-4108	*L. timidus* cut-marked bone	12110 ± 120	15350-14620 cal. BP (31.7%) 14375-13810 cal. BP (62.1%) 13735-13675 cal. BP (1.6%)

3.5 – *Radiocarbon determinations from human-modified bone and antler from Creswell* (M. Beresford. Source: Pike et al, 2007)

human occupation of the UK in the Aurignacian and Gravettian, the lack of convincing stylistic parallels for the Creswell art on sites of these periods on the continent, and the relative abundance of Creswellian occupation in the UK, it was felt the art was very likely to be of Late Magdalenian age'.[29] This theory led Paul Pettitt to surmise that the groups using Creswell were either the same or 'intimately connected' with those from Continental Europe,[30] a belief that the author shares wholeheartedly. In fact, I would go so far as to suggest that they probably were the *same* peoples, as shall be argued over the next few chapters.

So, returning to the point laid out above regarding the formation of the flowstone deposits, there was a specific method in which this could be used to date the engravings: 'the rock art at Creswell takes the form of engravings directly into the limestone bedrock...a number of the images were overlain by thin veneers of precipitated calcite (flowstone) which is datable by uranium series (U-series) disequilibrium dating'.[30] English Heritage were only too happy to fund this dating, stipulating that it must, however, be centred around 'identifying and accurately recording the engravings and determining their quantity, character, age and context'.[31] So, a series of samples were taken in the hope of verifying a date for the art. The interstratification of art and flowstone had successfully been used before at the French sites of Grande Grotte and Grotte du Cheval at Arcy-sur-Cure[32] but it was still an extremely rare process within the Palaeolithic world. U-series dating had also been used successfully at Covalanas, Cantabria, Spain.[33]

The results from the Church Hole U-series tests reflected a multi-phase development for the flowstone growth – the thicker flowstone gave a younger date whereas the thinner deposits showed signs of flaking and weathering (consistent with little or no recent deposition) and gave the oldest dates. It was hoped that the U-series dates would confirm a date of approximately 12,500-12,000 radiocarbon years, and undoubtedly the luck that surrounded much of the discovery held fast, as the approximation was indeed confirmed. The dates for the formation of the flowstone in both Church Hole and Robin Hood Cave came out consistent with a Late Upper Palaeolithic date, which tied in with radiocarbon dates from arctic hare bones associated with contemporary flints (within a date range of between 15,700-13,200BP). This also tied in with contemporary dates from other British sites such as Gough's Cave in Cheddar Gorge, Somerset, and provided a '*terminus ante quem* of 12,800 years before present, confirming the find as the first ever discovery of Palaeolithic cave art in the British Isles and the most northerly in Europe'.[34]

The results suggested that the Creswell engravings were indeed made in the Late Upper Palaeolithic, which corresponds with the stylistic interpretations (ie. Late Magdalenian). It is certainly possible that the art is earlier, perhaps Neanderthal (although art from this period is so far lacking), Early Upper Palaeolithic (attested by the leaf points in Robin Hood Cave) or Middle Upper Palaeolithic (the Font Robert points in Pin Hole) but all are extremely unlikely based on wider evidence. The art is therefore almost certainly of Magdalenian date and confirms the beliefs put forward by the discovery team.

Let us now discuss what this means for Creswell, and indeed for Britain, as part of a wider European culture. The most interesting aspect of the art relates to Paul Pettitt's (and also the author's) belief that the so-called 'bird' panel is actually a depiction of the

---

[29] Pike et al *Verification of the Age of the Palaeolithic Cave Art at Creswell Crags*, in Pettitt et al *Palaeolithic Cave Art*, p.35
[30] Ibid, p. 36-37
[31] English Heritage Research Agenda: *Creswell Crags ice age rock art*, http://www.helm.org.uk/upload/pdf/Research_Agenda2005.pdf
[32] Pike et al *Verification*, p. 37
[33] Ibid, p. 37
[34] English Heritage Research Agenda

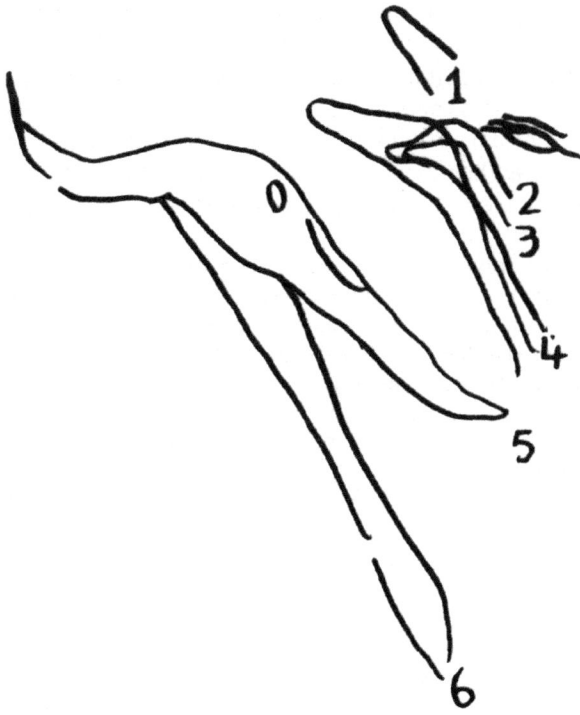

3.6 – *Church Hole Panel VII depicting, in the author's opinion, stylised female forms* (M. Beresford, redrawn from Pettitt 2007)

female form, if a little crude, based on wider examples. Pettitt argued against the art depicting birds thus: 'the similarity of the images and their spatial proximity suggests that they must be viewed and interpreted together, perhaps as a scene, and personally I find this mix of imagery within a scenic frame unlikely'.[35] He further explained that the Creswell 'birds' were unique within Magdalenian art – they are depicted as incomplete, long-necked, show no eyes or any attention to detail and are 'clustered' together. This is not the usual depiction within Magdalenian artwork. He also pointed out, quite successfully in the author's opinion, that because panels X and VII share a similarity in form we must assume that one or the other is upside down. As panel X is located at head height (in Creswellian / Magdalenian times) it seems highly improbable that this engraving is upside down. With panel VII the artist had to at least crouch due to the ceiling height, leading Pettitt to argue that they would most likely have had to lie down or stoop in a bent-over position using the opposite cave wall for support as there was probably not enough pressure necessary for engraving in the lying down position. During inspection of the cave, Roger Jacobi noted evidence of charcoal deposits within the Late Upper Palaeolithic layer just below the 'female' engravings which may suggest a small fire was lit in order to aid the engraving process.[36]

With the image turned upside down, then, images 2, 3, 4, 6 and particularly 5 look very similar to more wider continental images of stylised female figures. What the author finds of particular interest is the accentuated buttocks (with the Creswell engraving) but the lack of breasts when compared to earlier Palaeolithic female depictions, most notably the 'venus' figurines that date approximately between 30,000-20,000 BP. Traditionally they are seen as representations of the Mother Goddess or as fertility totems, but Pamela Russell has recently argued against this theory. She suggests that they do not necessarily reflect pregnant women, which would seem to suggest that they reflect obese women instead. Her theory is that it could have been possible for women to become obese when we consider diet and mobility, or lack of, during the over-wintering period. Here,

---

[35] Paul Pettitt *Cultural Context and Form of Some of the Creswell Images: An Interpretive Model,* in Pettitt et al *Palaeolithic Cave Art,* p. 125

[36] *Discovery, nature and preliminary thoughts about Britain's first cave art,* Pettitt, 2003, *Capra 5,* available at http://capra.group.shef.ac.uk/5/pettitt.pdf

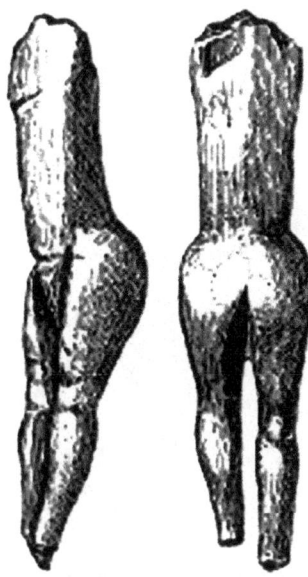

3.7 – *The Venus Impudique from the Dordogne*
(Public Domain)

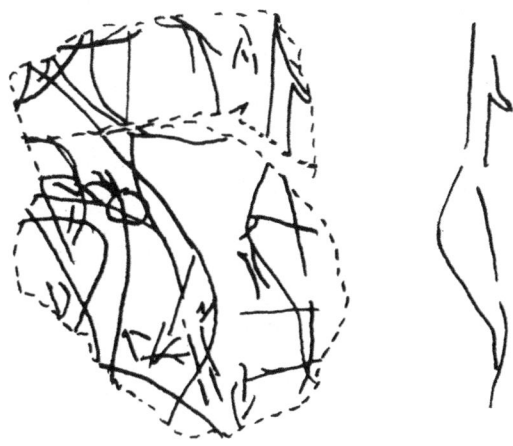

3.8 – *Gönnersdorf Plaquette 2, with detail of engraving 2b – Note the 'truncating' line at the bottom of the legs*
(M. Beresford, redrawn from Pettitt, 2007)

a lack of exercise and a relatively high-fat meat-based diet may, in her opinion, have caused an element of obesity but I would argue that this seems highly unlikely to cause such a vast increase in body weight in such a short period of time. Let us consider the first venus figurine, the 'Venus Impudique' discovered by the Marquis de Vibraye in the Dordogne in 1864, as this shares none of the 'traditional' venus figurine characteristics (ie. obese accentuations) but is markedly similar to the Creswell depictions.

Images 1-4 from Church Hole panel VII also share similarities with depictions from Gönnersdorf in Germany, and image 5 even has the truncating line at the bottom of the legs. As Pettitt argues, how likely are these similarities to have occurred by chance? He concludes that 'we should be more surprised if the Church Hole images really did depict (rare) birds rather than a very common cultural theme (in the Magdalenian)'.[37]

But what did this wider 'cultural theme' mean? Pettitt believes that 'aspects of the Creswell art and art of the continental Late Magdalenian indicate intimate conceptual connections across long distances which are suggestive of shared values about the Magdalenian world'[38] and, as it appears that the most plausible cultural association is with what Garrod termed the Creswellian (for Britain) and the wider continental Late Magdalenian (so 15,000-13,500BP) this appears to be the case. If the Creswell art is to be Britain's only example of cave art, then the question arises why Creswell? It may well be through shared association and its importance within the Magdalenian world, 'the importance of the gorge probably lies in that it was a reindeer migration route (in the period) between summer calving grounds towards the Peak District (of Derbyshire) and winter grazing towards Doggerland. There would also have been other resources in the area such as fur-bearing arctic hares'.[39] Bones of migrant geese found at the

---

[37] Pettitt *Cultural Context*, p.134
[38] Pettitt *Cultural Context*, p.113
[39] *Creswell Crags: Discovering cave art in Britain, Current Archaeology*, No. 197, May / June 2005

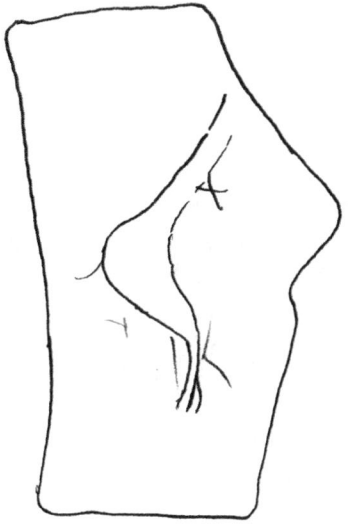

3.9 – *Engraving of a stylised female form on a lamp from the site of Grotte de Courbay* (M. Beresford, redrawn from Pettitt, 2007)

3.10 – *The sorcerer from Les Trois Freres* (Public Domain)

German Magdalenian sites of Gönnersdorf and Andernach seem to support this winter occupation and a journey over Doggerland to Creswell / Peak District in the summer.

It appears clear that Creswell fitted into a wider geographical exploitation in the period, but why one particular cave for the art? What was so special about Church Hole? One suggestion is that the north side of the gorge may have been seen as the land of the living (hence the habitation of Robin Hood Cave or Mother Grundy's Parlour) whereas the south side was something completely different[40] – are we suggesting it reflected the realm of the dead? If we consider that the majority of Late Upper Palaeolithic backed pieces came from the northern side of the gorge – 57 from Mother Grundy's Parlour, 40 from Robin Hood's Cave, 17 from Pin Hole with only 4 from Church Hole – we could take this to mean that the south-facing caves were chosen for habitation and these would obviously have made more pleasant camps, but in that case would we not expect the majority of artwork to therefore also come from these caves? As it is not, apart from the one example in Robin Hood's Cave and Mother Grundy's Parlour respectively, we must deduce that the Church Hole cave art was meaningful and representative in the period, even if that is now lost to us in the present. The question that arises is whether this signifies, perhaps, a spiritual divide between the two sides of the gorge.

There appears obvious parallels with the French cave sites of La Vache and Niaux in the valley of the Vicdessos river in Ariege, which also face each other.[41] Niaux has rich Magdalenian cave art but poor archaeology, whilst La Vache has a rich archaeological record and several pieces of mobile art and yet no parietal art. It is therefore interesting that the portable art from Creswell (authentic or not) came from all three north-side caves (Pin Hole, Robin Hood Cave, Mother Grundy's Parlour) but *not* from Church Hole?

---

[40] *Discovery, nature and preliminary thoughts about Britain's first cave art,* Pettitt, 2003, *Capra 5*
[41] Pettitt *Cultural Context*, p.118

Considering the mobile art from the Pin Hole for the moment, recent work to remove the graphite on the 'humanoid' engraving in the conservation department at the British Museum suggests that the outline may indeed be genuine but that certain details may be false, particularly the emphasised phallus.[42] Perhaps this 'de-sexing' now means it could fit in with more general representations of part-human / part-animal examples, although the 'sorcerer' from the site of Les Trois Freres that shows a human figure adopting the guise of a deer also has an obvious phallus depicted. Pettitt argues that this mobile art – that is the sagaie from Pin Hole and the rib engravings from Pin Hole and Robin Hood's Cave – hold clear continental stylistic links.[43]

Finally, then, regarding general Magdalenian art styles, what we generally note are only the head or forequarters being depicted. As Bahn stresses, European cave art tends to reflect this trend, with natural shapes in the rock being utilised by adding eyes, ears or muzzles.[44] So how does this compare to the Creswell art? Well, there are clear parallels with the continental art, in particular a further example of the 'famous phenomenon' from the French cave of Peche Merle, where a natural 'horse-head' shaped rock was used to depict a painting of a horse. At Creswell, a bison-shaped rock formation on the ceiling has clearly been modified to create an image of two superimposed quadruped heads.[45]

The evidence for the art at Creswell belonging to the European Magdalenian appears overwhelming, and this supports what re-analysis of past archival material alongside new discoveries had been suggesting. The art at Creswell now provides a solid foundation from which to hypothesise about what the archaeology is telling us. Britain is no longer comfortable with a separate 'Creswellian' tag, and as the next chapter shall show, nor should it be.

---

[42] Ibid, p. 120
[43] Ibid. p. 121
[44] *New discoveries of Cave Art in Church Hole (Creswell Crags, England), Antiquity,* Vol. 78, No. 300, June 2004
[45] Ibid.

4
Challenging The Creswellian: The Way Forward

'There seems little to invalidate the theory of the bridge of dry land, excepting the immense time which must necessarily have elapsed since England and the continent were joined; - more than one eminent geologist has held this opinion, which the arrangement of the strata on each coast fully warrants'

Thomas Bateman, *Vestiges of the Antiquities of Derbyshire,* 1848

As the above quotation shows, the early antiquarians had begun to understand that at one time in our distant past Britain had been not an island but an extension of Europe. When Thomas Bateman, famous for his 'barrow-digging' in the Peak District, was writing upon this theory of a land bridge the exploration of Creswell had not even begun. Here lies the foundation for the argument that 'Creswell Man' need not have been a localised inhabitant but rather part of a much wider European Ice Age world.

In the one hundred and sixty years since Bateman's *Vestiges* we have learnt that the people who visited Creswell came across this land bridge as part of a wider European community. They left behind in its caves evidence for their habitation in the form of flint tools, bone and antler artefacts and indeed in their artwork all of which, furthermore, reflect similarities with European examples. The general consensus now is that the Late Upper Palaeolithic peoples followed migrating animals along river systems from areas such as Belgium, Holland and Germany across Doggerland, down the Trent and on through the higher grounds of the Magnesian Limestone plateau by using the natural gateway of Creswell Crags (we can also note a similar exploitation of the landscape at Continental 'valley' sites such as at Vézère and the Dordogne in France). They then moved further west into the Peak District in late spring / early summer to exploit the reindeer before heading south to the Cheddar Gorge in Somerset. The cyclical journey was completed with a trip back over Doggerland for the winter.

In essence then, we are looking at a seasonal occupation of Britain rather than a prolonged habitation. For Creswell, this most likely meant a stop-off of perhaps six or seven weeks, perhaps even by a small hunting party rather than a whole group or tribe. This seems to be supported by the lack of large Creswellian 'open sites' in Britain (as opposed to the opposite on the Continent) and also the tight cluster of radio carbon

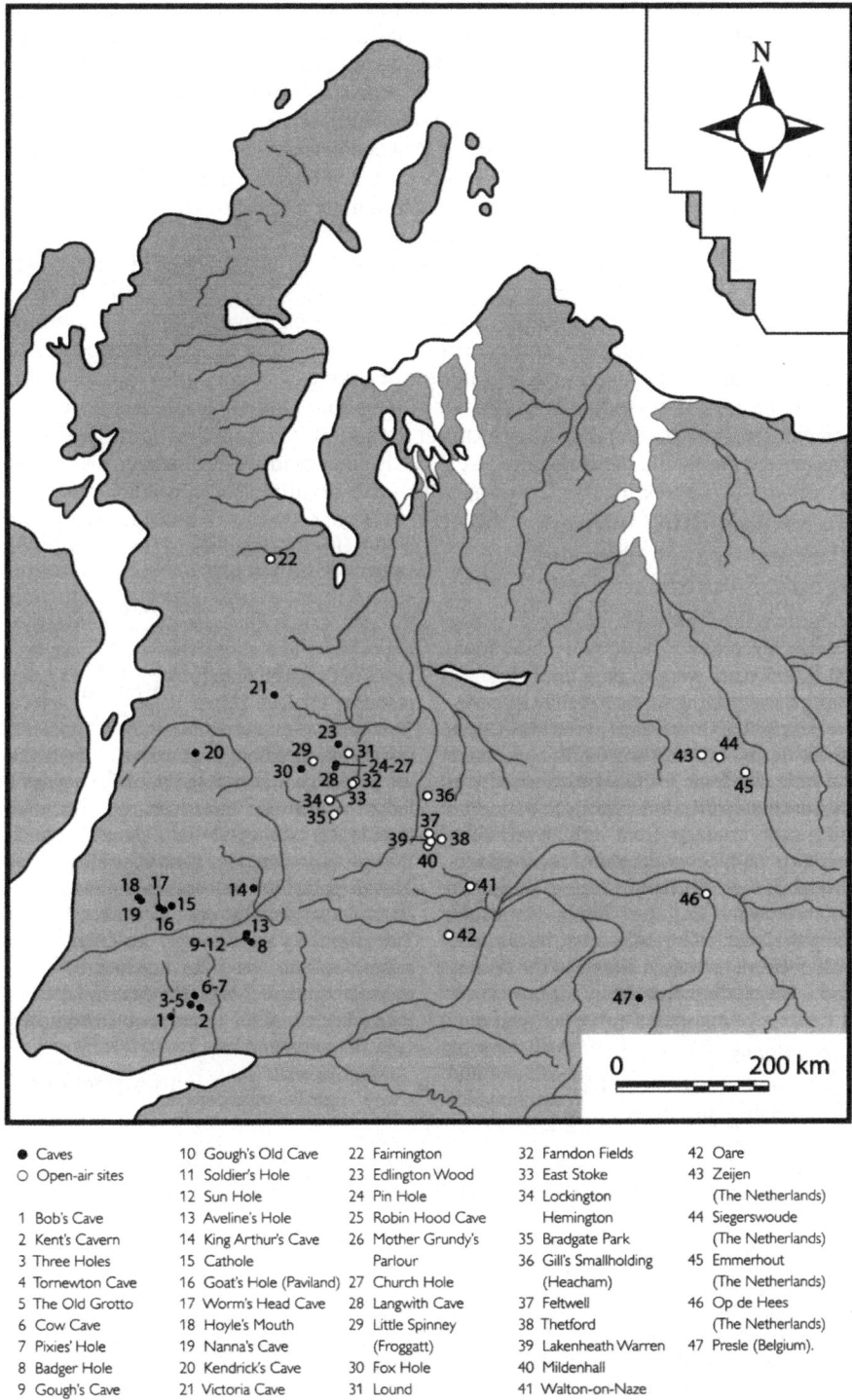

4.1 – *Distribution map reflecting Late Upper Palaeolithic sites contemporary with the Creswellian occupation at Creswell Crags* (after Jacobi & Pettitt, 2009)

dates for the period.[1] Despite this rather sporadic use, Garrod chose Creswell Crags as her type-site for her 'Creswellain' model, as has been discussed, but it may be worth at this point considering the flint assemblage in more detail, given the current research on this subject. Garrod based her theory on the single and double obliquely truncated backed pieces (Creswell and Cheddar points) but as Jacobi[2] has noted this theory is full of discrepencies. It is also worth pointing out that when Cheddar and Creswell points occur together on British Late Upper Palaeolithic sites, Cheddar points always outnumber Creswell points (ironically even at Creswell Crags itself). Perhaps therefore we should be discussing a 'Cheddarian' rather than a 'Creswellian'!

For all sites with either Cheddar or Creswell points (or both) we have quite conclusive dating samples (from radiocarbon dating) of between 12-13, 000 radiocarbon years ago. However, considering certain samples from Robin Hood Cave at Creswell obtained by Campbell in the 1970s, we can note certain difficulties. Although the number of backed pieces are small, and indeed rather fragmentary, we can nevertheless ascertain that all but one are almost certainly from Creswell / Cheddar points.[3] Radiocarbon dates from these contexts correlated with a Late Upper Palaeolithic date, which adds weight to the suggested typology of the flints, and yet there is clear evidence for a much earlier faunal assemblage mixed in with the later deposits – 'observations on typology, raw materials and preservation types confirm a background noise of Middle Palaeolithic artefacts mixed with those clearly of a Late Glacial age'.[4] What this suggests is difficult to understand, but it may relate to a final mixing of deposits at the end of the last Ice Age. Even the term 'point' may be a misnomer as although Bohmers[5] termed the label 'Cheddar point' for the trapezoid backed pieces that Garrod offered up as the link between the Early Upper Palaeolithic (Aurignacian) and the Late Upper Palaeolithic (Creswellian), recent work by Jacobi[6] has shown that through 'use-wear' analysis it is possible to demonstrate that the flints were side-mounted (ie. as a blade) rather than tip-mounted as was initially thought.

Largely through Roger Jacobi's work on the subject, we can confidently put forward a typological model for 'Creswellian' flints:[7]

1 – trapezoidal backed blades with a double truncation (Cheddar) and backed forms with a single truncation (Creswell)
2 – end scrapers on long blades
3 – burins, mostly on prepared truncations
4 – piercers and *becs*
5 – Magdalenian blades, truncated blades with heavily worn ends and splintered pieces
6 – well-made blades and bladelets detached from cores with a single preferred flaking direction

---

[1] see Pettitt, *Cultural Context and Form*, in Pettitt, Bahn & Rippoll *Palaeolithic Cave Art at Creswell Crags in European Context*, (Oxford) 2007, p. 115
[2] Roger Jacobi *The Creswellian, Creswell and Cheddar*, in *The Late Glacial in North-West Europe: human adaptation and environmental change at the end of the Pleistocene*, CBA Research Report No. 77, (1991), pp. 128-40, Eds. N Barton, A J Roberts & D A Roe
[3] Ibid, p. 134
[4] Ibid, p. 136
[5] Bohmers, A *Statistics and graphs in the study of flint assemblages: II A preliminary report on the statistical analysis of the Younger Palaeolithic in northwestern Europe*, Palaeohistoria, 5, 1956, pp. 7-25
[6] Jacobi, *The Creswellian*, p. 131
[7] Creswellian flint typology adopted from Barton et al, *The Late-glacial reoccupation of the British Isles and the Creswellian*, Journal of Quarternary Science, (2003), 18 (7), pp. 631-43

We can, however, see that although initially regarded as the 'type fossil' for a Late Upper Palaeolithic culture, the Creswell point has now been shown to occur in Final Palaeolithic 'Federmesser' contexts (such as at Pixie's Hole, Devon) and in assemblages with straight-backed blades being the dominant tool such as Hengitsbury Head, Dorset. Should it now be seen as a link between the Late and Final Upper Palaeolithic rather than as a defining cultural facies?

Clearly, then, the Creswellian model is proving less and less relevant for Britain, but what of its wider links to the Continent? Were the Creswellian tools merely an imagined variant of a wider cultural assemblage suggested by Garrod? The answer to this is proving problematic, largely due to the difficulties in strictly defining European variants – the terms 'Cheddarian' and 'Creswello-Tjongerian' perhaps hindering rather than aiding the clarification process. As early as 1963 Bohmers[8] noticed what he believed was an obvious 'cultural dichotomy' that showed 'striking points of resemblance between the Creswellian and a wide range of continental sites from Belgium to Holstein'. More recently Stapert and Johansen[9] have shown that the site at Zeijen in the Netherlands offers clear evidence of Creswellian flints, with six Cheddar points and ten Creswell points recovered during fieldwork there. They also found an associated ring of stones that were deemed to be a tent base with a hearth approximately 2m from the entrance. Might this suggest that the site was another of the temporary settlements used by a hunting party on its way from Europe into Britain as part of a wider yearly cycle?

Recent work in Sweden has suggested that within the Late Upper Palaeolithic the temperature did not rise on the same scale as that in Britain, most likely due to the adjacent land ice. This is supported in the fact that mammoth remains were recovered from Lockarp in south-west Scania with an approximate date of around 13,360BP, long after the mammoth had disappeared from Britain.[10] Much of Larsson's work has hinted at temporary, small-scale camp sites similar to those in and around Holland, Belgium and Britain. The difference, however, is the presence of tanged points

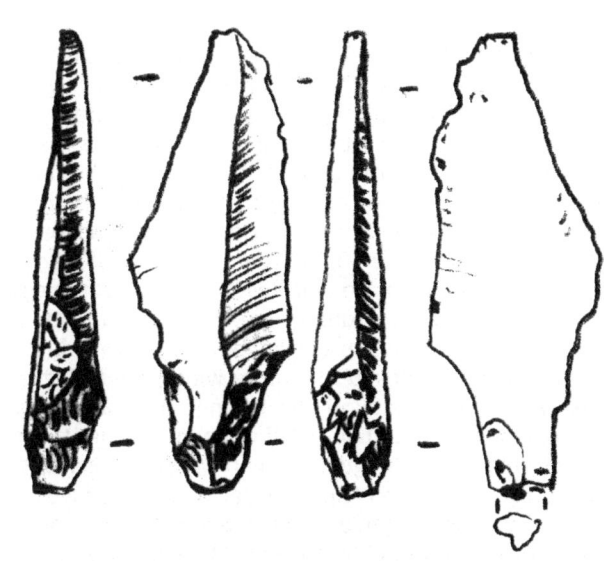

4.2 – *Tanged point from Röke, Sweden*
(M. Beresford, redrawn from Larsson, 1991)

---

[8] A Bohmers *A statistical analysis of flint artefacts* in Brothwell, D & Higgs, E *Science in Archaeology,* 1963, pp. 469-81

[9] Stapert, D and Johansen, L *The Creswellian site at Zeijen* in *Patina: Essays presented to Jay Jordan Butler on the Occasion of his 80th birthday,* Metz, WH, van Beek, BL, Steegstra, H (eds.) Metz, van Beek & Steegstra: Amsterdam / Groningen, 2001, pp. 503-526

[10] Lars Larsson *The Late Palaeolithic in southern Sweden: investigations in a marginal region,* in *The Late Glacial in North-West Europe: human adaptation and environmental change at the end of the Pleistocene,* CBA Research Report No. 77, (1991), pp. 122-27, Eds. N Barton, A J Roberts & D A Roe

generally deemed to be arrowheads and similar to the Danish 'Bromme points'. Larsson has further noted that many of these tanged points have been recovered from the inlets and outlets of lakes (which is also typical of Danish finds) but also in valleys. How integral the hunting of reindeer in the region was at this time is unclear – bone and antler artefacts have been noted but these may well be of a Late Boreal date and further work is needed on the subject. As he summarises, many of the flint finds from the Swedish west coast may relate to a distinct regional variation of a Late Upper Palaeolithic tradition. Given the presence of mammoth, the climatic changes in the region and the uncertainty as to how much reindeer and elk were exploited, is it any wonder that tool types were modified to meet changing demands? Due to the harsher landscape and climate ' hunting based on reindeer and elk must be pursued in rather different ways, and accordingly calls for the flexible organisation of society. Furthermore, the position of sites next to the inlets or outlets of lakes indicates that fishing, for example of salmon, may have been a major activity'.[11] Were the tanged points a direct response to this and therefore a necessary regional variant?

The question arises, then, as to whether we are looking at (as Garrod argued) localised industries or rather regional *adaptations* of a wider culture in response to particular challenges in a given locale, ie. differing landscapes and therefore hunting methods or even subtle differences in the quality or composition of raw materials. Lewis-Williams[12] theorised on how far the aesthetic qualities of flints affected decisions behind the construction of specific tools – 'many writers point out that some of the tool types, such as the finely made and highly standardised Solutrean points, go well beyond functional necessity' – in other words it was the *shape* of the tool as opposed to solely its *function* that began to matter. If this is the case, does this then lend weight to Armstrong's beliefs that the inhabitants at Creswell were influenced by Solutrean hunting parties (see Chapter Two)? I would agree that aesthetics began to play a part in society's psyche, but this can be seen much earlier than the Late Upper Palaeolithic. With the arrival in Western Europe of the anatomically modern humans (*homo sapiens sapiens*) we can see the importance of aesthetics being developed in factors such as the burial of the dead with grave goods, body ornamentation, decorative 'belongings' and indeed in art itself, and this a good 30,000 years before the 'Creswellian'. Lewis-Williams is not to be dissuaded though, as he believes 'Upper Palaeolithic tool shapes varied frequently both geographically and through time: the shapes of one's stone artefacts signalled one's social group'.[13] I am not convinced. On paper this theory *could* support the idea of a Creswellian as opposed to a more widespread Magdalenian, but given the evidence of Creswell-type tools found on sites in Holland and Belgium there is clear indications that the inhabitants of Britain could be found further to the east, but more convincingly the heavy presence of Magdalenian artefacts at Creswell proves the settlement (if sporadic) by European peoples. Here I refer to the engraved horse rib bone from Robin Hood Cave, the Pin Hole man engraving, the decorated bone implements and most notably the Church Hole artwork itself. If Magdalenians were using the Creswell caves at the height of the 'Creswellian', where on earth were the Creswellians themselves? The argument for a series of socially distinct cultural groups operating in a relatively small area just does not stack up, to my mind.

Even over the last twenty years or so the shift in thinking has changed dramatically. And yet much of the information was there all along. As Jacobi[14] stresses 'there can be little doubt that the study of museum collections is unfashionable, and this clearly

---

[11] Ibid, p. 126
[12] David Lewis-Williams *The Mind in the Cave: consciousness and the origins of art,* 2008, p. 75
[13] Ibid, p. 76
[14] Jacobi *The Creswellian,* p. 128

shows in much that is written about our past...contrary to popular belief, the uniqueness of caves as repositories of information on early man was fully appreciated even very early on...these observers made every attempt to record their work. The total of resulting publications is prodigious, although most recent researchers have done little to seek these out'. As has been shown in the first two chapters of this work, this early information is invaluable to our understanding of Creswell Crags. But there is only so much we can do with the material recovered from the site in the last 130 years or so, and although 'undoubtedly (it can) make significant contributions to an understanding of broader aspects of the palaeontology and archaeology of the East Midlands, the present database offers very little beyond "probabilities" when it comes to attempting the definition of individual Late Upper Palaeolithic toolkits'.[15]

In order to obtain a clearer picture, both locally and more wider afield, we must consider further the archaeology of the region. As part of the North Derbyshire Archaeological Survey in the 1970-80s Clive Hart and his team discovered a possible Palaeolithic open camp-site in the fields above Mill Farm, Scarcliffe / Whaley. Hart commented at the time that in all 384 flints were noted in the plough soils and that although much of the material was of a rather poor quality some of the later pieces were comparable to those from Mother Grundy's Parlour at Creswell, and that they were of a narrow blade type flint industry.[16] The flints discovered are represented in Fig. 4.4.

Hart believed that the concentration of flints suggested an open camp-site of Late Upper Palaeolithic / Early Mesolithic date and that it probably related to the two cave sites at Whaley (Whaley Shelters I & II). However, Jacobi[17] believes that Hart was mistaken in his interpretation of the flints and that the site is rather of a Late Mesolithic date at the earliest and could even be Neolithic. That the site had been subjected to heavy ploughing even by the early 1980s means that today nothing will remain of any potential archaeology located there, which is unfortunate as the site is the only known open site in the region.

However, to the south of Creswell a number of these open camp sites are emerging such as those at Farndon Fields near Newark in Nottinghamshire, which is just 33km south of Creswell and had a flint scatter of around 15 hectares (dominated by end scrapers), and at the site of Newtown Linford, Leicestershire. Should we now see Creswell as a seasonal camping ground in later Prehistory where hunting parties sought refuge, while the main group lived in a larger, open site? It would then be these smaller hunting parties that we are seeing within the archaeological record at the caves at Creswell and the surrounding area.

A series of seasons of fieldwalking at Farndon Fields between 1991-94[18] recovered a great number of flints, and gave evidence for flint knapping as the full range of debitage was recovered as well as a variety of tasks using / manufacturing tools, with long end-scrapers and points present. As the report details, for a fieldwalking project the results were exceptional as almost no damage had occurred to the retrieved material through ploughing, etc, and the site was then the only known Creswellian open camp in northern and western Britain. As Jacobi[19] stresses with Farndon Fields its close proximity to Creswell Crags must mean that there was some definite link between the two, particularly as the flint evidence suggests a different use (for Farndon). The dominance of end scrapers could suggest that prey was taken back there to be processed, while the

---

[15] Ibid, p. 136
[16] Clive Hart *The North Derbyshire Archaeological Survey* (Sheffield), 1984, p. 19
[17] Roger Jacobi, pers. comm. July 2008
[18] see preliminary report *Farndon Fields: outline of the Late Upper Palaeolithic activity*
[19] R M Jacobi *The Stone Age archaeology of Church Hole, Creswell Crags, Nottinghamshire*, in Pettitt, Bahn & Rippoll *Palaeolithic Cave Art at Creswell Crags in European Context*, (Oxford) 2007, p. 103

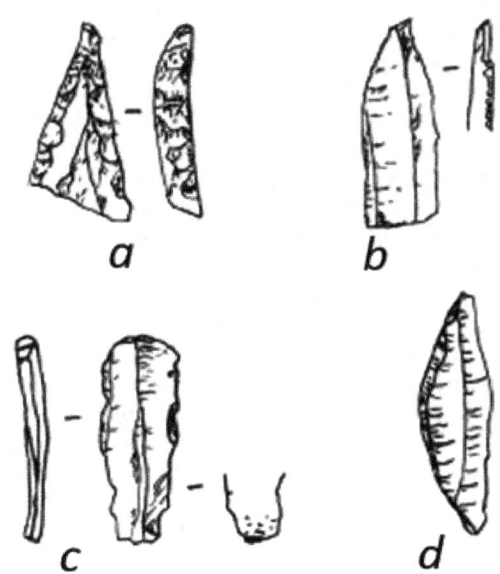

4.3 – *Flint tools from Newton Linford: piercer (a), obliquely truncated blade with burin scar (b), retouched blade with en éperon preparation (c), Cheddar point (d)*
(M. Beresford, redrawn from Cooper, 2002)

wider dominance of 'tool kit' type flints at the Creswell caves and the presence of sewing kits (discussed shortly) suggests the belongings of highly mobile inhabitants just passing through. It is certainly a convincing argument, and considering the contemporary, but more importantly, *local* sites appears to suggest this. From a geographical perspective we can note that almost all lie on the peripheries of river systems, and this cannot be coincidence. Even on a local scale within the Creswell Heritage Area, the majority of Ice Age cave sites all lie on the rivers Poulter and Wollen, and this seems to reiterate the point discussed earlier that the river systems were integral to navigation methods.

From around 450 worked flints recovered from the site at Newtown Linford a variety of traditionally accepted 'Creswellian' tools were apparent, chiefly six blades with *talons en èperon* (an obvious Creswellian characteristic), a Cheddar point, four burins, a micro-piercer, six broken piercers and a truncated blade with a heavily-worn end.[20] Many more stray finds have been recovered in this area over the last 15 years such as the backed blade from Lockington-Hemington (1995) and a convex-backed blade from Castle Donnington (1997).[21] So it seems the Creswellian hunters were utilising the local area, and this most likely fits into an even wider national, and indeed continental, landscape.

The importance of reindeer appears integral to the 'Creswellian' period. We have mentioned that the Creswell hunters moved on towards the Peak in order to exploit the spring-time calving and clear evidence for this comes from Ossum's Cave in the Manifold

---

[20] Lynden Cooper *A Creswellian campsite, Newtown Linford* in *Transactions of the Leicestershire Archaeological and Historical Society*, 76 (2002), p. 78
[21] Lynden Cooper & Roger Jacobi *Two Late Glacial finds from north-west Leicestershire* in *Transactions of the Leicestershire Archaeological and Historical Society*, 75 (2001), p. 118

Flint Type	Quantity
Cores	25
Core Trimmings	21
Waste Flint	178
Waste Chert (Brown)	1
Waste Blades	41
Waste / Hinge Fractures	12
Black Chert Blades	1
Snapped Blades	30
Utilized Blades	22
Utilized Flakes	5
Obliquely Blunted Creswell Points	2
Microliths (Rods)	3
Scrapers – Flint	15
Scrapers – Volcanic Stone	1
Hollow Scraper	5 + 1?
Burins	19
Hammer / Strike-A-Lights	2
Total	**384**

4.4 – *Flint tool types from the open site at Mill Farm, Whaley*
(M. Beresford. Source: Hart, 1984)

Valley. Here, nearly all of the reindeer remains recovered from excavation (predominantly teeth and antler) reflect a death for the animal at around 10-11 months.[22] This in itself seems to suggest that there was a clear targeting of the reindeer young, perhaps as they would be more vulnerable than the more mature reindeer. It is therefore not surprising that the main image within the Creswell art is that of a red deer stag.

The importance of deer within early human hunting was not lost with the transition of the Palaeolithic into the Mesolithic period. Evidence from Star Carr, North Yorkshire has shown that Mesolithic hunters were using the site as a temporary, open camp from about 8770BC in order to hunt immature deer in late spring / early summer. This mirrors the scene of our Creswellian hunters just four thousand years earlier. What is interesting to note is that around twenty-one pieces of perforated skull and antler fragments have been found at Star Carr. The suggestion is that they may have been worn as a 'headdress' in some form of ritual or worship, or perhaps even as a hunting disguise.[23]

One of the other main animals to be exploited at Creswell Crags in the Late Upper Palaeolithic was the arctic hare, as has been discussed. This is a far cry from the more easily associated fauna of the woolly mammoth, traditionally associated with Ice Age hunters. Indeed, even as recently as 1977 Campbell[24] attributed the bones of reindeer, horse, woolly mammoth and woolly rhino to the Creswell hunters. Charles and Jacobi[25] however have shown that by analysing cut-marks on animal bone it is clear that the trapping of arctic hare was by far the most dominant faunal exploitation at Creswell, with all the radiocarbon dates clustering around 12, 700BC. As Steve Mithen explains, Creswell man knew 'how to extract sinews from a hare to use as sewing thread, how to turn its leg bones into awls and needles, how to make socks, mittens and coat lining from the fur'.[26]

---

[22] Bramwell, D et al *Ossom's Cave, Staffordshire: A study of its Vertebrate remains and Late Pleistocene Environments*, in *Staffordshire Archaeological Studies*, 4, 1987, pp.25-59
[23] see J G D Clark *Excavations at Star Carr*, (Cambridge) 1954, A J Legg & P A Rowley-Conwy *Star Carr Revisited*, (London) 1988
[24] J B Campbell *The Upper Palaeolithic of Britain*, Vol. I, (Oxford), 1977
[25] Charles, R & Jacobi, R *The Late Glacial fauna from the Robin Hood Cave, Creswell Crags: a re-assessment*, in *Oxford Journal of Archaeology*, 13 (1994), pp. 1-32
[26] Steve Mithen *After the Ice: A Global Human History, 20,000-5,000 BC*, (London), 2003, p. 117

4.5 – *The arctic hare was integral to the lifestyle of Creswell Man*
(© Robert Nicholls, www.paleocreations.com)

Interestingly, the exploitation of arctic hare is apparent from the early antiquarian work of Mello and Boyd Dawkins, and while Mello mentioned in his reports on the Church Hole excavations that human-modified hare bones were recovered from the same layers as quartzite tools, Boyd Dawkins amended the context they were found in as he was obviously troubled by this apparent contradiction – how could Late Upper Palaeolithic worked bone be from the same context as Middle Palaeolithic quartzite tools? Whereas Mello stated they were found in Layer 4, Boyd Dawkins altered this to the upper cave earth sediments. It is unfortunate that we will probably never know whether this was an initial error on Mello's part, or whether Boyd Dawkins opted for the more accepted view (we will remember Boyd Dawkins was not adverse to these kind of errors; the mis-attribution of the laurel leaf point relating to the skeletal remains from Robin Hood Cave to the Neolithic period springs to mind – see next chapter). Either way, the notion that the upper most layer – the stalagmitic breccia – within Church Hole had numerous hare bones is interesting as exactly the same occurrence was noted in the breccia layer in Robin Hood Cave. As Jacobi[27] reminds us, Campbell noted further hare bones from his excavations outside Robin Hood Cave and again they had signs of being worked by humans. In fact Church Hole, Pin Hole and Robin Hood Caves all harboured identical examples of pointed tibias of mountain hare, as did Gough's Cave at Cheddar, and all are deemed to be bone awls.

That these examples date to the Late Upper Palaeolithic has been shown through radiocarbon dating, but exactly when did the use of materials other than stone occur?

---

[27] R M Jacobi *The Stone Age Archaeology of Church Hole, Creswell Crags, Nottinghamshire,* in Pettitt, Bahn & Rippoll *Palaeolithic Cave Art at Creswell Crags in European Context,* (Oxford) 2007, p. 77

There is much debate on this issue. Mithen[28] believes that the Neanderthals did not use raw materials such as bone, antler, ivory or wood and yet Lewis-Williams[29] argues for the opposite: that Neanderthals did in fact use these materials but did not exploit their malleability. Without doubt the modern humans used them in abundance at Creswell, but what about the Neanderthals? It is curious that amongst both Mello and Boyd Dawkins' early work and Armstrong's later work there appear examples of worked bone or antler artefacts that appear to come from Neanderthal contexts. Again, is this an error on the archaeologists' part, or perhaps a gross mixing of sediments most likely by glacial waters? Although I cannot be certain, I would lean towards the latter of the two.

There is a good example from Creswell that may shed some light onto this debate. Throughout the Upper Palaeolithic world there is clear evidence that its people collected animal teeth – including fox, wolf and bear – and carefully bored through them in order to make necklaces. Let us take the Macharoidus tooth from Robin Hood Cave. Could this be very early evidence of a 'possession' but perhaps lacking the cognitive processes needed to transform it into an adornment? Put another way, was it deemed to be something special by the ancestors of the Creswellian owner who lost or hid the tooth around 13,000 years ago, but who lacked the thought patterns to transform it into something other than a mysterious object? Whatever the Pin Hole man engraving represents, are we here also seeing a much earlier object 'transformed' into something mystical in later Prehistory, given that the rhinocerous bone itself predates the engraving by some 20,000 years? Or perhaps they fit into another notion that may have been developed in the Upper Palaeolithic: that of social networking. If we consider the evidence for artefacts such as worked shells or beads, we could attribute them to some form of trade network due to their widespread occurrences. This need not reflect long-distance movements by *peoples,* it may simply represent the artefacts themselves travelling over vast areas. The piece of amber found in Robin Hood Cave throws up parallels with this, as the nearest natural resource would be the Baltic. The early antiquarian Rooke Pennington[28] mentions a piece of amber found at the Creswell caves, and although he does not mention the cave itself, in all likelihood it was Robin Hood Cave. Further examples from Upper Palaeolithic levels have been noted at Gough's Cave, Somerset and at Star Carr, Yorkshire.[29]

It is difficult to appreciate the thought processes behind this 'ornamentation' by using the modern mind. Colin Martindale[30] explains that 'we need to understand the "irrational" thought of the poet as well as the rational thought of the (laboratory) subject solving a logical problem...we need to investigate the historical evolution of ideas in the real world as well as how concepts are formed in laboratory situations. Finally, we must ask how emotional and motivational factors affect cognition'. If we can adopt this mentality then entirely new possibilities emerge. Take the so-called horse pendant from Church Hole cave. It has been discussed earlier that initial ideas deemed the artefact to be some form of pendant, or possibly a serrated edge flesher and given its size it would certainly be useful on smaller mountain hare pelts[31] but recently Jacobi has come up with a more novel (and I might suggest correct) idea. He suggests that it could in fact be a thread-winder and that it may relate to an Ice Age sewing kit along with the bone needles and awls found in the cave.[32] If we consider the fact that Boyd Dawkins found one needle in 1876 and Thomas Heath found another in 1879, we could question as to

---

[28] Rooke Pennington *Notes on the barrows and bone caves of Derbyshire* (1877), p. 102
[29] see J Wilfrid Jackson *The Creswell Caves, Journal of the British Scientific Association,* Vol. VI, No. 41, 1967, pp. 8-23
[30] Martindale, C *Cognition and Consciousness*, (Homewood, Illinois), 1981, viii
[31] see Campbell, 1977, Jacobi, 2007
[32] see Jacobi *The Stone Age Archaeology of Church Hole,* p. 97

whether there was in fact a cache left in the Church Hole, particularly poignant due to the lack of occupation evidence from the period.

At Church Hole, Jacobi also questioned the three pieces of worked antler that Garrod believed were all from the same artefact (see chapter two, this work). He offered the idea that they may in fact be from two separate artefacts and compares them to the example found in 1977 by Bramwell at the cave site of Fox Hole at Wheeldon in the Derbyshire Peak. This example is very similar to that from Creswell and another example from the German site of Stellmoor, although that artefact is slightly shorter. His belief is that they may have had small flints attached to the 'scoop' or 'groove' at one end and were in essence small projectiles. The author recalls a stray find of a Creswell point found near to the Neolithic tomb at Minning Low in the Peak and interpreted at the time as a 'missile' by Clive Hart as part of his 'North Derbyshire Archaeological Survey' in the late 1970s / early 1980s. So Jacobi's theory is certainly an interesting one, and again shows how ideas on the period are constantly changing.

To summarise this Late Upper Palaeolithic use at the Church Hole, particularly by contextualising the artwork and the artefacts recovered there, we can see that only a few flint tools were recovered and we have to wonder as to whether they were used in the engraving of the art itself. We also have the possible 'sewing kit' and some charcoal evidence that is obviously indicative of fires. So does this evidence relate solely to the engraving of the art and whatever temporary settlement may have been linked to it? It certainly seems to suggest a markedly sporadic, probably seasonal, habitation most likely by passing hunting parties, but not on the same scale as the caves on the opposite side of the gorge. Church Hole's Late Upper Palaeolithic archaeology is almost certainly Magdalenian in culture and although I would argue that this most likely applies to the site of Creswell as a whole in this period, there is another niggling possibility that harks back to the early theories put forward by Armstrong, and that is what if the two sides of the gorge were seen as separate locations but not for the reasons assuaded to already in this work. What if, rather, Church Hole was almost an Ice Age hotel, designated for travellers passing through the region, whilst the northern caves were inhabited by the locals? For example, what if local 'Creswellians' lived in the northern, Derbyshire side caves and our Magdalenian visitors stayed in Church Hole on the southern, Nottinghamshire side. Is that why we get art, almost exclusively, in Church Hole cave alone? It is possible, yet I would suggest highly unlikely. It is much more likely that there was seen as some clear divide socially and psychologically between the two sides of the gorge, and that is reflected in the archaeology and habitation of the caves.

A social and psycological divide relates to Lewis-Williams' theories discussed above on some form of shared social cognitive belief system. As he explains with the idea of the Neanderthal mindset, it must relate to the levels of consciousness which, although we possess the same mind structure as the 'Creswellians', it is proving extremely difficult for modern man to worship in what Mithen termed the 'cathedral' of their mindset: 'without the developed memory and the kind of fully modern language that must attend it, they (the Neanderthals) were unable to enter into long-term planning, categorize generations and human relationships in order to initiate complex kinship and political systems, and speak of and construct mental 'scenes' of past and future times. They were almost there – but not quite'.[33] And this proves the difficulty in us, in the present, understanding the early beliefs and social consciousness of the Late Upper Palaeolithic inhabitants at Creswell.

Our understanding of the history of Creswell Crags is at its highest level yet. The next step is to pass this information across to the widest possible audience. The aim

---

[33] Lewis-Williams Mind in the Cave, p. 285

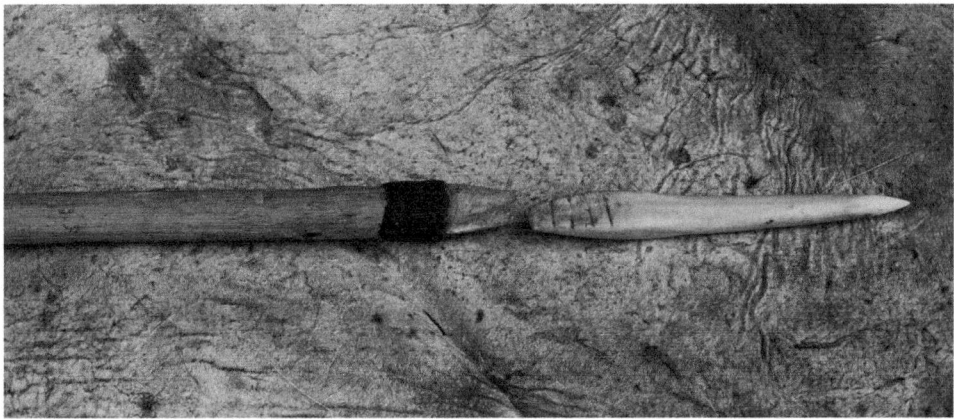

4.6 – *Engraving the bone point with incised lines helped to hold the projectile in place when hafted*
(© Creswell Heritage Trust)

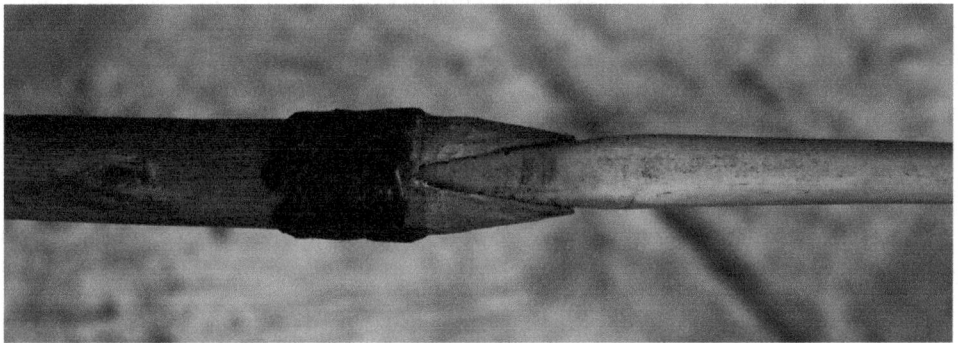

4.7 – *The hafted weapon*
(© Creswell Heritage Trust)

of the Creswell Heritage Trust is clear on this point: 'together with site and collections management, education and visitor services are the most important activities of the Trust. Educational projects aim to promote the use of archaeology as a means of delivering a wide range of formal and informal educational objectives'.[34] Many of these educational projects have been developed in line with the National Curriculum – hundreds of school children visit the Crags each year – and resources are also applicable to colleges and universities as well as local history groups and Community projects. So we are certainly using this new understanding to promote Creswell's place within a wider context back in the Late Ice Age.

But are we any closer to understanding the Ice Age people themselves? I think we are. In order to do this it is important to lose the modern mindset and try and think like Creswellian man, and one of the best ways to do this is by studying children. In children we have an obvious window into the early stages of the development of cognitive thought processes, the exact same development that early man would have had to have gone through. From watching my own daughter and understanding how she looks at things in a different way to adults, and how she grasps simple, everyday occurrences it

---

[34] Creswell Heritage Trust website - http://www.creswell-crags.org.uk/virtuallytheiceage/index.html

becomes more productive in attempting to understand early man. Steve Mithen[35] gave an example of how he was playing with his three year old son, Nicholas, one day who was placing his plastic toy animals onto his zoo when he asked Nicholas if he should put the seal in the lake. His son eyed both the toy and his father for a moment and then replied 'yes. But actually it's a walrus'. Here we have a clear example that children soak up useful knowledge and retain it, in this instance with a meticulous knowledge of animals. And that can lead us quite nicely on to Creswell Man and his knowledge of animals, something that is attested to by the art within the Church Hole. Whereas in the present we have so much knowledge within our brains it is sometimes difficult to retrieve that, life in the Ice Age was in many ways less complex. I would argue that the natural world was, in essence, the 'beating heart' of Ice Age life; to put it simply, they lived by the land and died by the land and this may well go some way to explain the importance of caves. For caves could be seen as a natural extension of the natural world in that by going into a cave a person was, for all intents and purposes, entering into the Mother Earth. A cave was Mother Earth's shelter, a place to 'offer up' the dead and send the soul back from whence it came and, perhaps with Church Hole, a place to worship that Mother Earth. Perhaps the animal engravings were a symbolic gesture of thanks for providing the hunters with food and perhaps the stylised female engravings were a celebration of her. We will probably never know for certain, but to my mind it is as good an argument as any.

In the final stages of writing this book new dating evidence was published for some of the human remains from Gough's Cave, most notably for the cut-marked skull, which is discussed in more detail in the next chapter. Previously, radiocarbon dates had given a time span of between 15,500 - 13, 500BP but this new evidence gives a much more precise date of 14,700BP.[36] What this means is that we now have a more precise date for the recolonisation of Britain after the Last Glacial maximum, a date that is some two thousand years before the artwork at Creswell. Clearly, as new evidence emerges it will continually improve our understanding of this part of our past, and this has been the picture we have seen throughout the course of this book.

So can we now confidently say that Garrod's term the 'Creswellian' and her idea of a localised British culture is no longer applicable? I think we can. The more we have understood the archaeology the clearer this has become, even dating as far back as Mello's engraved horse rib bone with its 'Magdalenian spirit'. The flints are not the same as their European counterparts, that much is granted, but they may perhaps reflect a localised *adaptation* rather than a definitive *industry*, and this seems to be supported by the other artefacts of Magdalenian design. Here I refer to the bone implements and the mobile art – should Armstrong's anthropomorphic figure be viewed along the same lines as continental art that depicts man emulating beast (such as the sorcerer from Les Troire Freres) but also the later example of Prehistoric man attempting to take on the guise of an animal at Star Carr?

Finally, this issue of Creswellian vs Magdalenian should be conclusively addressed by the engraved art at Creswell, particularly in the form of the stylised females as with these we have a direct link with the European Magdalenian. The proof is there for all to see and we can no longer question it. Perhaps it is finally time for Britain to forget that it is an island and accept its position as part of an Ice Age European Union, if not in our present then certainly for our past.

---

[35] Steve Mithen *The Prehistory of the Mind,* (London) 1998, p. 32
[36] R M Jacobi & T F G Higham *Quaternary Science Reviews,* (in press)

5
The development of Creswell as a heritage site: a 21ˢᵗ century perspective

> *'It is daybreak on a winter's day in 12,700BC...looking down among pine and birch that have found shelter in the gorge. Its sides are peppered with fissures and caves. Wisps of smoke wind their way between the trees...a fireplace smoulders at the entrance to the cave'.*
>
> Steve Mithen, *After the Ice*

This is the scene at Creswell Crags in the Late Upper Palaeolithic around the time the cave art was being engraved. The past 130 years of evolving exploration and analysis has allowed us to confidently interpret what life was like in the Ice Age. We now know that prior to around 60,000 years ago no human presence existed in the gorge and the changing climate saw an initial fauna of hippo and rhino give way to a more arctic assemblage including reindeer, mammoth and arctic hare. Indeed, archaeology has shown us that at the time of the art's engraving these arctic hare were being exploited far more than the woolly mammoth that is perhaps more easily associated with the Ice Age. The pelts would have made warm clothing, the sinews used for thread, the meat as a food source. The Creswellian (or perhaps Magdalenian) people of this period were not the first to inhabit the caves, with evidence stretching as far back as to just before the Last Major Glaciation – the Devensian – where Neanderthals occupied the area. People still flock to Creswell Crags in the present, attracted by its beauty and tranquility but also, thanks to this past exploration, for its history. For, as the current publicity leaflet informs us, Creswell has been 'inspiring visitors for over 50,000 years'.[1]

Just like any site it was always going to prove a huge issue as to how to manage Creswell as a heritage site. The decision in 1976 to put retaining gates on the cave entrances was hugely controversial, with many local people annoyed that they were no longer able to gain entry to what they saw as their caves – many had played in the caves

---

[1] *Creswell Crags: Inspiring Visitors for over 50,000 years,* Publicity leaflet to coincide with the opening of the new Museum and Education centre, June 2009

64 BEYOND THE ICE

5.1 – *The merels boards from Church Hole cave*
(M. Beresford)

when they were children. It is easy to empathise with both sides of the argument: the caves had harboured evidence from all periods of history, with the obvious Palaeolithic remains but also Mesolithic flints at Mother Grundy's Parlour and Neolithic pottery. Most of the caves that were excavated also revealed later occupation – Bronze Age pottery and metalwork, human remains dating to the Iron Age and artefacts dating to the Roman period all being present. Excavations at Church Hole in 2008 revealed a large limestone block incised with a pair of merels boards for the Medieval game Nine Men's Morris where players use counters to attempt to make a line of three (or 'mill') in which case the opposing player would lose one of his pieces.[2] Boyd Dawkins mentioned a bone counter discovered in this same cave during his excavations[3] although he attributed it to the Roman period, but with the discovery of the Medieval game it could well now be linked to this.

So it is therefore easy to empathise with the locals, who see the closure of the caves (apart from guided tours) as ending this historical legacy. On the other hand, if the caves had not been sealed off how would the archaeology and the preservation of the cave interiors be faring with open access for all? If we consider the cave site of Langwith Bassett, around 3 miles south of Creswell and incorporated within the Creswell Heritage Area, where Palaeolithic remains were uncovered by Mullins in the early 1900s and Armstrong in the 1920s we can see the way the Creswell caves may have ended up. Access to the cave is still open, although it is on private land, and it has been used for

---

[2] Hall, M A & Pettitt, P B *A pair of merels boards on a stone block from Church Hole cave, Creswell Crags, Nottinghamshire, England,* 2008, a preliminary paper held by the Creswell Heritage Trust
[3] Boyd Dawkins, W *On the mammal fauna of Creswell Caves,* 1877, *Quaternary Journal of the Geological Society,* Vol.33

5.2 – *The cave at Langwith Bassett, where Armstrong discovered Palaeolithic remains in the 1920s*
(M. Beresford)

'recreational purposes' – graffiti adorns the cave walls and empty beer cans litter the floor. A recent study[4] looked at identifying local cave sites and how to manage these, so perhaps some time in the near future Langwith Bassett cave, along with similar cave sites, will be protected in the same manner as the Creswell caves.

The story of Creswell's development as a heritage site begins, quite surprisingly, alongside the early exploration of the site in the 1870s. The earliest recorded visit to the Prehistoric caves comes from *The Derby Mercury* of 9th October, 1878 which informs us of an excursion by the Students' Association of an unknown London university: *'a large number of students assembled at the Victoria Station, where they were met by the Rev. J. Magens Mello who had kindly consented to conduct the party to the justly celebrated bone caves of Cresswell'*.[5] There followed a tour of the caves and a lecture on the excavations by Mello, culminating in 'an excellent tea of ham and eggs' provided by Mr Woodhead.

A further early visit is detailed in the *Daily News* of 25th August, 1879[6] where we are informed that Boyd Dawkins himself led a group from the British Association on a historical visit to several sites in the area, including the excavations at Creswell Crags (which the Association were funding), after which they journeyed to Roche Abbey and

---

[4] Davies, G, Badcock, A, Mills, N & Smith, B *The Creswell Crags Limestone Heritage Area Management Action Plan,* 2004, Unpublished, ARCUS, Department of Archaeology, University of Sheffield
[5] *University Students' Association. Excursion to Cresswell* in *The Derby Mercury,* Wednesday 9th October, 1878, Issue 854
[6] *The British Association at Sheffield,* in *Daily News,* Monday 25th August, 1879, Issue 10405

on to the Neolithic henge of Arbor Low in the Peak District. Further detail of this visit appeared two days later in *The Derby Mercury*:

> 'the party which went to Creswell Crags on Saturday (23rd) had a most enjoyable and instructive outing. It was originally intended to limit the party to 100, but the known picturesqueness of the chosen locality induced such a plentitude of applications that the Committee of Management decided to extend the number'.[7]

The Crags were described in the programme as being a romantic glen in the Permian rocks, a fitting testament to the way they captured the imagination of the early visitors. By 1912 the site was recognised as an Ancient Monument:[8]

5. *List of Ancient Monuments* – The Committee recommended the County Council at their last meeting that a list of Ancient Monuments be prepared, and the following list has been supplied by the Thoroton Society, a copy of which has been sent by the Society to H.M Commissioners of Works...

Object	Locality	Notes
Creswell Crags	Creswell	A passage through rocks made by the River. Bones of antediluvian animals found here
Half in Derbyshire		
Half in Nottinghamshire		

A number of letters exist, from members of the British Association, the Welbeck Estate and local societies and Committees, that highlight the concern regarding the number of intruders to the caves, which appear to range from 'hooligans' bent on causing damage to 'persons unknown' who it appears were carrying out their own personal excavations. An insight into these 'hooligans' comes from 1959 when we hear how 'on Saturday March 7th two youths (colliery workers) were found using hammers to damage the interior of Pin Hole cave'.[9] The Welbeck Estate seemed keen to prosecute but were unsure how to proceed in this, quoting the Ancient Monuments Act, 1931: 'any persons acting in contravention of the provisions of this subsection shall be liable on summary conviction of a fine not exceeding one hundred pounds, or to imprisonment for a term not exceeding three months, or to both'.[10]

Mentioned in 1955 was the need to replace the wooden gate (on Pin Hole cave), which intruders were continually breaking through, with a steel grille, and a further letter from Armstrong himself to a Mr. Elliot of the Welbeck Estate in 1957 states that 'Messrs. Steel, Peach & Tozer of Rotherham' had offered to provide the necessary steel to construct the grille.[11] A letter from the Welbeck Estate to the Ministry of Works dated 1st January 1959

---

[7] *The British Association in Derbyshire*, in *The Derby Mercury*, Wednesday 27th August, 1979, Issue 8591
[8] Nottinghamshire County Council Minutes (printed), Finance Committee 30th January 1912 p.39 (Notts Archives)
[9] Letter from the Welbeck Estate to the Ministry of Works, 17th March, 1959 (Ref. B.7/28, TNA)
[10] Ancient Monuments Act, 1931, Section 6 (sub-clause 2)
[11] Copy of a letter between A Leslie Armstrong and Mr. N E Elliot of the Welbeck Estate Office dated July 31st, 1957, held at The National Archives, Kew (part of the Creswell Crags letters collection, no ref. given)

clearly states the Duke of Portland's support in erecting a grille and stressed that the grille had been constructed and was ready to fit.[12] It appears that the point in question, however, was the dispute between local archaeologists and the Welbeck Estate, as the former wanted a foundation base for the grille of a 3ft high brick wall, whilst the latter argued that this would detract from the 'natural' appearance of the caves.

It is hard to believe then that a final decision on the way forward for Creswell Crags took so long to be implemented. Not until the 1970s did we see any real heritage management take place. A meeting in January 1970, including members of both Nottinghamshire and Derbyshire Planning Departments, the Welbeck Estate and a number of Museum Organisers, drafted a list of requirements but highlighted that there were concerns over funding, which bodies would be involved and ultimately who would govern the site. The key issues were:

- Church Hole open to the public, all other caves, closed by grills, to be available only on request to Welbeck Estates
- A car park with small information / toilets building, preferably using the sewage disposal works access
- A Warden Service to control public use and check trespass, damage, etc;
- No public access to the Crags north of the Creswell Road

One of the key stipulations was that there was to be 'no commercialisation - ice creams, etc (unlike the site at Arbor Low in the Peak District) which would be available at Creswell in any case'.[13]

In 1975 the Derbyshire and Nottinghamshire County Councils jointly took on the lease of the site from the Welbeck Estate and opened up the site as a 'picnic area'. The following year, metal grilles were finally fitted to all of the cave entrances in order to limit entrance and a small visitor centre was opened. The purpose of the centre was to 'provide visitors with high quality scientific information and to assess and consolidate the site's scientific significance'.[14] Basically, to promote access to the site and to raise awareness of its significance. The scheme was largely successful as it became a Site of Special Scientific Interest (SSSI) in 1981 and a Scheduled Ancient Monument in 1985.

The centre was also aimed at addressing the ad hoc site tours that the resident gamekeeper had been running since the 1960s.[15] Rogan Jenkinson was appointed Ranger of the site and his work led to an extension of the centre in 1979 and his collaboration of past work and his own research was published in 1984.[16] This led to the Prehistoric Society putting forward the proposal to make the Crags a World Heritage Site in 1986, but the bid was rejected on three points:

1) The presence of inappropriate infrastructure at the site, namely the sewage works
2) The presence of the B6042 road running through the centre of the gorge
3) The inadequate state of the visitor centre

---

[12] Letter from the Welbeck Estate to Mr. C R Wright of the Ministry of Works, dated 1st January, 1959, Ref. No. AM3/6675 (TNA)
[13] Note of a meeting held at Gedling House on 20th January, 1970 (Ref. A20, TNA)
[14] *Creswell Crags Museum & Archaeology Park: A Potted History of Creswell Crags and the Heritage Trust, Business Plan – Appendix 4*, 2003, Section 1.3
[15] Maria Smith (Creswell Heritage Trust), pers. comm, June 2009
[16] Jenkinson, R D S *Creswell Crags: Late Pleistocene sites in the East Midlands*, BAR British Series 122 (Oxford), 1984

5.3 – *1980s publicity leaflet showing early interpretations of how 'Creswell Man' may have looked* (© Creswell Heritage Trust)

Later that year the *Creswell Crags Heritage Area Strategy* was outlined to tackle these three problems as well as providing a focus for future work and management of the site, and in 1990 the Creswell Heritage and Groundwork Trusts were set up to implement the proposals, later splitting in 1994 with the Creswell Heritage Trust left to manage the site.[17] In 1995, David Bellamy (who became Patron of the Trust) launched the *Creswell Initiative*, the final phase of the proposals, and Severn Trent Water began a £4.2m project to relocate the sewage works. Three years later Redland (Lafarge) began proposals to relocate the through road and work was finally completed in 2006. Trent & Peak Archaeology performed the watching brief on this development and noted a number of 'debris-choked fissures, fissure caves and gulls (one of which) contained rounded erratic pebbles, which were presumably glacially or periglacially derived'.[18] This highlighted the potential of there being further caves or fissures in the area that may contain Pleistocene material. A number of flint artefacts were also recovered, most dating to the Neolithic and Bronze Ages, but also including two Mesolithic microliths (as at Mother Grundy's Parlour), a broken flake or blade with a striped yellow patina (which Jacobi[19] stressed is only noted on Lower or Middle Palaeolithic pieces so appears to suggest an earlier human presence in the area than the archaeology so far noted at the Crags) and a crested blade with cortication that may offer a Late Upper Palaeolithic date, although as Jacobi further points out it may equally be Neolithic.

The third point was finally addressed with the proposal, and subsequent funding, of a new £4.5m Museum and Education centre. As the Business Plan stated 'Creswell

---

[17] *Creswell Crags Museum & Archaeology Park*, 2003, Section 1.3
[18] *Creswell Crags, B6042 Crags Road Diversion Scheme (SK 533743)*, Trent & Peak Archaeology Report, *Derbyshire Archaeological Journal*, Vol. 127, 2007, p. 122
[19] Ibid. p. 123

Crags has suffered from poor and unsympathetic management in the past, and present management and interpretation are inadequate to protect and conserve the site in the public interest in the long term'.[20] The launch in 2001 of the now award-winning website *Virtually the Ice Age*[21] at the British Museum created highly positive reviews and visitor numbers to the website soon peaked at around 30,000 hits per month. However, it was still a 'virtual' museum and could never be expected to make up for the lack of an adequate centre in the long term. The construction of the new centre coincided with the writing of this work, and although delays to its opening meant that it was impossible to consider its impact in terms of increased visitor numbers and so forth, it nevertheless creates an exciting new chapter for the site and is a positive step for the future.

In an article in the *Worksop Guardian* just prior to the centre opening, we were informed that Creswell Crags had remained 'something of a mystery to generations of local people' and that Prehistory in general was often misconstrued (even by this article I might hasten to add): 'it (Prehistory) started with the Romans, took a brief look at Stonehenge and that was about it'.[22] As the Roman period effectively *ended*, not started, the Prehistoric period, it is somewhat clear exactly why a new education centre was needed. Creswell Heritage Trust's former director Nigel Mills had previously explained that a 'lack of investment and modernisation at the original visitor centre had severely limited its ability to live up to its reputation as one of Britain's top heritage sites'.[23] One of the aims of the new centre is to provide a focal point for Britain where people from all over the world can learn about the Ice Age, a factor which will be aided by certain museums agreeing on short and long term loans for some of the important artefacts discovered at the Crags. Locally, both Derby Museum and the Brewhouse Yard Museum in Nottingham have agreed to loan artefacts, whilst the British Museum of London have also come on board, with hugely significant artefacts such as the incised horse rib bone artwork being placed on temporary display, yet another testament to the international importance of the site.

The building itself was opened on June 27th by Sir David Attenborough and will provide an epicentre for Ice Age research and education. The new building has a specially designed collection room for storing and preserving artefacts, an archive room for the rich collection of journal articles, newspaper cuttings, books and theses on the site and a lecture room, all of which will aid future work, education and promotion of the Crags. This should be the final stage in the site's quest for World Heritage Status, putting it on a par with Stonehenge in Wiltshire and the Pyramids of Egypt.

So how does Creswell Crags fit into the wider picture? The only other comparable site, and development of this nature, is that of the similar gorge at Cheddar in Somerset which attracts around ½ million visitors each year[24] (Creswell's visitor figures are reflected in the table below, with a notable increase in 2003 onwards when the cave art was discovered). Guided cave tours run into Gough's Cave and there is also a museum and visitor centre. The archaeology of the caves at Cheddar is similar to Creswell, although a burial – a complete skeleton of a young male dated to the very early Holocene, that is just after the final ice retreat – was discovered in 1902.[25] This could be one of the reasons why visitor numbers are so high as the marketing potential of a burial is huge (there is a reconstruction of the skeletal remains 'in situ' in the cave itself, with a reconstructed model in the visitor centre reflecting how the 'Cheddar Man' may have looked).

---

[20] *Creswell Crags Museum & Archaeology Park*, 2003, Section 1.1
[21] *Virtually the Ice Age:* http://www.creswell-crags.org.uk/virtuallytheiceage/index.html
[22] *New £4.5 million visitor centre opens at Creswell Crags,* in the *Worksop Guardian,* 8th May, 2009
[23] Ibid.
[24] The British Mountaineering Council website: http://www.thebmc.co.uk/Feature.aspx?id=1843
[25] Chris Stringer *Homo Britannicus*, (London), 2006, p. 141

5.4 – *Exhibition space inside the new visitor centre* (© Creswell Heritage Trust)

Year (April to April)	Number of Visitors
1998/99	2239
1999/00	1807
2000/01	1148
2001/02	1282
2002/03	1692
2003/04	2818
2004/05	4922
2005/06	4132
2006/07	3056
2007/08	3286

5.5 – *Visitor figures for Creswell Crags, based on adult visitors undertaking guided cave tours. The low figure for 2000/01 reflects the outbreak of Foot and Mouth disease, with the centre closed for 3 months during the epidemic. As predicted, visitor numbers soared after the discovery of the cave art for the following two seasons, and have noticeably tailed off since. Although remaining higher than figures prior to the art, this can be explained by the additional cave tour of Church Hole to incorporate the art's discovery.* (M. Beresford. Source: Creswell Heritage Trust)

THE DEVELOPMENT OF CRESWELL AS A HERITAGE SITE   71

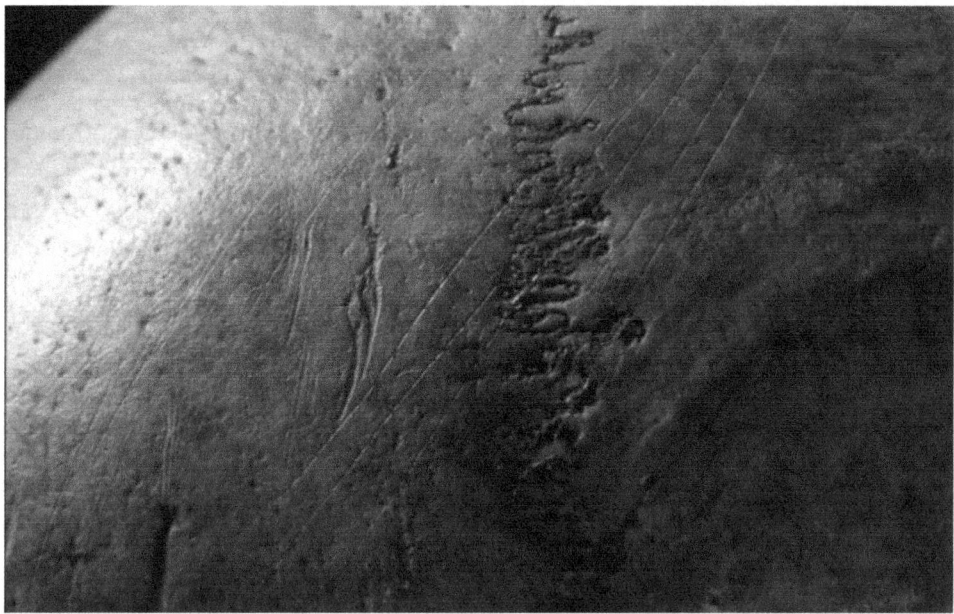

5.6 – *Skull of the Cheddar Man. Cut marks on the skull are clearly visible to the left of the suture* (© Natural History Museum)

There are also other human remains from Gough's Cave, notably the skulls of another adult and a child but also other skull fragments, jaw bones and teeth. Rather disturbingly, but also quite attractive from a tourist point of view, one skull fragment showed clear signs of cut marks made by flint tools.[26] These remains were so well preserved that when the skull was reconstructed it showed that it had been held in the left hand of the person holding it while a stone tool in the right hand had effectively scalped the head and cut through the muscles holding the lower jaw.[27]

Here was possible evidence of cannibalism. The press had a field day, running headlines such as *'Stone Age Brits ate kids'* and *'What they Gorged in Cheddar'*.[28] It is beyond the scope of this book to discuss this theory in any great detail, but the point to glean from the situation is that headlines, even macabre ones, mean increased visitor numbers (as we saw with the Creswell cave art). If Creswell were to have had a burial there would this have enriched the story, and thus the visiting experience? It is difficult to say given the location of the two sites, Cheddar lying in easy reach from London and other more southerly tourist spots, Stonehenge for example. It is also true that Creswell has often been overlooked due to its location within the heartland of the coalfields, an area tarnished by the view that it is set within a bleak and unsightly industrial conurbation, particularly after the demise of British industry. However, it is worth discussing the human remains from Creswell at this point, remains that are often overlooked in the larger picture.

Campbell[29] noted a marked difference in burials between the Early and Late Upper Palaeolithic in Britain, with seven in the Early and 105 in the Late. This would seem

---

[26] Ibid. p. 141
[27] Ibid. p. 141
[28] Ibid. p. 14
[29] J B Campbell *The Upper Palaeolithic of Britain*, Vol. I, (Oxford), 1977, p. 160

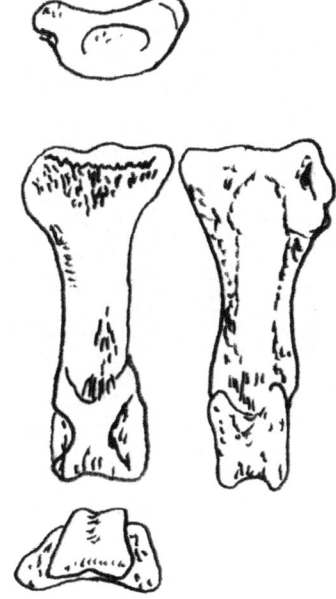

5.7 – *Fossilised lynx phalanges from Pin Hole* (M. Beresford, redrawn from Brothwell, 1981)

to suggest a clear emphasis between the two periods on burial rites and practices, and we could therefore assume, for a site such as Creswell, that contemporary human remains should be present. We have already detailed the remains from Armstrong's Pin Hole excavations analysed by Brothwell (see Chapter 2, this work) but it is worth commenting here on the discrepancy between Brothwell's four bones and Jenkinson's six. Both Jenkinson[30] and Campbell[31] mention the same four bones as Brothwell[32] with the addition of two phalanges deemed to be human. In a later work, Brothwell[33] clearly states that although initially deemed to be human (and published as thus) they are in fact of fossilised lynx. Curiously, this work was first published *before* either Campbell or Jenkinson offered their belief on the matter, and neither mention the possibility that it could be animal bone.

Jenkinson further discusses the remains as being quite well-preserved, and that the juvenile frontal fragment (Brothwell's LL1628) is fractured extremely squarely which he believes makes it difficult to attribute as being natural breakage or post-mortem. All the remains were discovered between 13-20m from the cave entrance and within a Late Palaeolithic context (based on artefact assemblage). Jenkinson further points out these remains appear to fit into a wider context within British Late Palaeolithic sites where human bones are noted that have been broken into smaller pieces post-mortem (such as at Gough's Cave), leading him to suggest that they 'may indicate ritual activity involving human corpses', although not as extreme as Campbell believes.[34]

By far the main cave in terms of human remains at Creswell is that of Robin Hood Cave (perhaps understandable when considering this cave houses the most human occupation evidence). Campbell recovered human remains from his own excavations in the cave in 1969, namely a frontal fragment of a skull, from the undisturbed layer OB. He found further remains in the 19th century spoil, and although clearly from a disturbed context, firmly believed that all came from a single individual. The evidence does seem to confirm this, for example skull fragments 130, 131 and 153 all fit together as do other remains including jaw fragments and a molar tooth that clearly comes from this jaw. Analysis has determined that the individual was an adult male, between 23-30 years of age.[35]

Associated remains date the frontal (and therefore possibly all the remains) to the Late Last Glacial with floral and faunal remains pinpointing this to Zone II or the Allerød

---

[30] R D S Jenkinson *Creswell Crags: Late Pleistocene Sites in the East Midlands,* (Oxford), 1984
[31] Campbell *The Upper Palaeolithic*, 1977
[32] letter between Don Brothwell and Dr. Owen of University Museum, Manchester dated 14th February 1962 (Armstrong Collection, Creswell Heritage Centre)
[33] D R Brothwell *Digging up Bones, 3rd Edition,* (London), 1981
[34] Jenkinson, *Creswell Crags*, p. 81
[35] Campbell, *Upper Palaeolithic*, p. 218

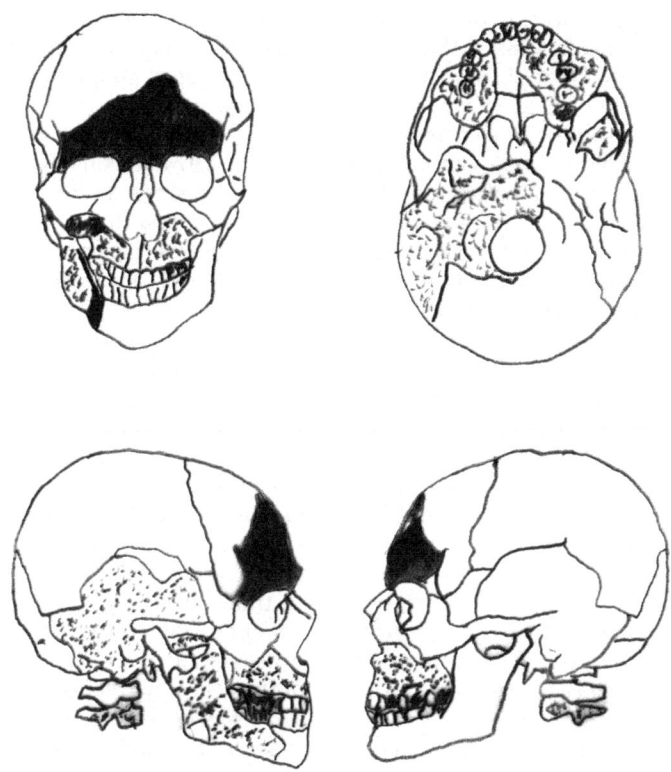

*5.8 – Skull fragments found at Robin Hood's Cave in 1969, layer OB and E
(M. Beresford, redrawn from Campbell, 1977)*

interstadial. However, a radiocarbon date from *Equua Przewalski* (wild horse) came out at only 10,390 ± 90 years BP (which suggests a Zone III date).[36] Clearly the dating is less than conclusive. The fact that there appeared no evidence of a complete burial led Campbell to argue that the skull may have 'served as a trophy...eventually (being) ceremonially shattered, perhaps after it had been suspended or mounted to ward off the enemy'.[37] This is pure speculation on Campbell's part and there is no evidence to support this theory, nor for his claims that the absence of a vault for the skull could be indicative of cannibalism. He bases these theories on a comparison with the Boro tribe of South Africa, where 'prisoners are taken and carried off by the victors (whereby) the adults are killed and eaten at the dance feast'.[38] Images of Armstrong's anthropomorphic figure 'dancing a ceremonial dance' are conjured by this theory, but it is difficult to make cross cultural comparisons here and perhaps Campbell was clutching at proverbial straws when he claimed the 'victim' was of prime 'warrior' age. Also, the ample faunal remains associated with layer OB clearly indicate that food shortage was not an issue in terms of a forced cannibalism (if that were what we were dealing with) and again this is the same scenario we find at Gough's Cave.

---

[36] Ibid. p. 219
[37] Ibid, p. 219
[38] Ibid. p. 220

Jenkinson[39] also discusses human remains from his excavations in the 1970s, but also those found by Laing in 1889.[40] These are described as being, from the rear chamber, a cranial fragment and a fibula associated with 'canine of bear, chopped bones, choppers and scrapers of the rudest Acheulian type'.[41] This would appear to suggest a much earlier date than Upper Palaeolithic. In the Western chamber a radius and a humerus were discovered alongside Palaeolithic artefacts. In 1974 Jenkinson found a human mandible in the stratigraphic layer left by Laing in the Western chamber, which Oakley[42] documented as having a nitrogen content (1.1%) consistent with a Devensian age. Laing at the time believed the remains in the Western chamber were part of a complete burial but that they were probably later in date due to the suggested Neolithic date, by Boyd Dawkins, of a 'spearhead' associated with the remains.

Jenkinson agrees with the 'complete burial' theory but suggests an Upper Palaeolithic date – there is no evidence to suggest the context was disturbed (meaning Laing was excavating an in situ deposit) and the Neolithic 'spearhead' may well have been a laurel leaf point. Oakley also applied nitrogen testing to Campbell's remains from Robin Hood's Cave, finding levels between 3.81% and 4.12%, which quite clearly differ greatly from that of the 1974 mandible. These remains are well preserved, whereas the mandible is 'highly eroded by root action and not heavily fossilised'.[42] It therefore seems they must be from separate skeletal remains, and if the date of 10, 390 BP is accurate, further attests to the earlier date for the mandible and Laing's remains (although these are now lost so cannot be verified). In conclusion then, there are two (probable) Early Upper Palaeolithic individuals from Laing's excavation and two later individuals in the form of the cranium (Late Upper Palaeolithic) and the other remains (possibly Flandrian).

Finally, let us consider the remains from Mother Grundy's Parlour, where we must return to the skull found by Mello and Boyd Dawkins in 1877. The reader will recall that Boyd Dawkins questioned the possibility of a Palaeolithic date for the skull (see Chapter 1, this work) but Jenkinson put paid to these doubts: 'there seems little doubt today that the skull was in situ, particularly as the overlying depth of sediment which was in contact with the roof argues against any localised disturbance'.[43] He therefore offers a Late Upper Palaeolithic date for the skull based on the stratigraphy and that the further remains discussed by Boyd Dawkins (in 1877) of at least three juveniles all from the red sandy cave earth could also be of Late Upper Palaeolithic or even Mesolithic date. Yet again, this is based solely on supposition and is far from conclusive. The only other human remains from Mother Grundy's Parlour came from Armstrong's work where he noted a single adult upper canine, and as this is now lost it is impossible to comment upon, save from the fact that it may atest to a further human skull, although it is just as likely that it could simply be a stray tooth.

There is certainly the possibility that one or more of the Creswell caves may at one time have housed Palaeolithic burials. Whether these were in fact complete burials similar to Gough's Cave remains uncertain, but there does seem to be a large proportion of skull remains apparent compared to other remains. From the table (Fig. 5.9) we can see that in each cave at least 50% or more of the human remains from Creswell included skull fragments, and from this we could interpolate this to suggest that perhaps

---

[39] Jenkinson *Creswell Crags*, p. 50
[40] R Laing *On the bone caves of Creswell and the discovery of an extinct Pliocene Feline (Felis brevirostris) new to Great Britain, Reports to the British Association for the Advancement of Science*, (Newcastle), 1889, pp. 582-84
[41] Jenkinson *Creswell Crags*, p. 50
[42] K P Oakley *Relative dating of the fossil hominids of Europe, Bulletin of the British Museum of Natural History Geology Series*, Vol. XLI, (34 (1)) (London), 1980, pp. 1-63
[43] Jenkinson *Creswell Crags*, p. 51

Cave	Number of separate 'burials'	Detail	Excavation	Number of remains including skull fragments	Percentage of human remains with skull fragments
Pin Hole	4	1) Temporal (skull frag) 2) Ilium (hip bone) 3) Clavicle (shoulder) 4) Skull frag	1) Armstrong 2) Armstrong 3) Armstrong 4) Armstrong	2	50%
Mother Grundy's Parlour	5	1) Skull & mandible (jaw) 2) Frags (unknown) 3) Frags (unknown) 4) Frags (cranium) 5) Tooth	1) Mello & Dawkins 2) Mello & Dawkins 3) Mello & Dawkins 4) Mello & Dawkins 5) Armstrong	3	60%
Robin Hood's Cave	3	1) Skull frags 2) Cranial frag (skull) & fibula (lower leg) 3) Radius (lower arm), humerus (upper arm) & mandible (jaw)	1) Mello & Dawkins / Campbell 2) Laing 3) Laing / Jenkinson	3	100%

5.9 – *Table showing human remains from the Creswell caves (M. Beresford)*

there is some form of ritualistic practice occurring. This need not be 'head hunting' or cannibalism as suggested by Campbell or Jenkinson, but it is worth noting that some of the other caves within the Creswell Heritage Area also harboured evidence of 'skull burials', chiefly Whaley II Rock Shelter and Langwith Bassett Cave, while other human remains were evident at the Sepulchre Cave at Markland Grips, nr Clowne and at Ash Tree Cave at Whitwell.

Clearly, the cave sites in the entire area held some spiritual purpose in relation to the dead within Prehistory, although radiocarbon dating tends to suggest it is later Prehistory, rather than the Palaeolithic, that saw cave burials. Nevertheless, the author is not dissuaded from believing that more ought to be made of the Creswell human remains, particularly when one considers that all remains came from the three Derbyshire-side caves (much like the portable art we must recall) and not the Nottinghamshire-side cave of Church Hole. Clearly this strengthens the argument that the two sides of the gorge were seen as being separate, but if the Nottinghamshire-side was deemed the realm of the dead (as Pettitt suggested, see Chapter 3, this work) and the Derbyshire side occupational / realm of the living, it begs the question as to why the burials should all

Site	C^{14} BP	Lab no.	Period
MGP	4640± 70	OxA-2350	Neolithic
	3790± 70	OxA-2351	Neolithic
	3720± 80	OxA-4442	Neolithic
	2210± 80	OxA-1832	Iron Age
RHC	5000± 40	OxA-7386	Neolithic
	4870± 120	OxA-1807	Neolithic
	2020± 80	OxA-736	Iron Age
	1785± 50	OxA-6851	Romano-British
Ash Tree	3730± 90	OxA-4446	Neolithic
Whaley	3470± 65	OxA-4021	Early Bronze Age
Langwith	2330± 60	OxA-2232	Iron Age
Markland Grips	4760± 90	OxA-4447	Neolithic

5.10 – *Radiocarbon dates from Human remains in the Creswell Heritage Area*
(M. Beresford. Source: Chamberlain, 2007)

take place here. One gets the feeling that we still do not fully understand the use and purpose of the caves and that Creswell still has secrets to offer.

This notion was proved in 2008 when excavations on the spoil heap outside Church Hole revealed an as yet undiscovered cave directly beneath the present cave. Poignantly named 'The Crypt' initial investigation of the cave seemed to suggest in situ, undisturbed Pleistocene deposits, confirmed by the discovery of a flint Cheddar Point and other artefacts very close to the entrance. Paul Pettitt explained that the cave is 'clogged with sediment (up to 2m deep) but stretches back several metres into the cliff... (the Cheddar Point) firmly identifies the assemblage as Late Magdalenian'.[44] And this mirrors the comments made above by Trent & Peak as part of the watching brief on the new road development – that the area may still have fresh caves awaiting discovery. An application to English Heritage to excavate the new cave is currently underway and could provide a revolutionary insight into Creswell Crags. The fact that a new cave, or possible extension or new chamber within Church Hole, has been found on the Nottinghamshire-side where we no so little in terms of use is potentially groundbreaking and may help unravel the final mysteries of the gorge.

Ironically, Armstrong suggested way back in 1924 that 'because of past exploration by antiquarians, archaeologists, treasure hunters and 'cabinet collectors' alike, the prospect of finding an undisturbed site at Creswell appeared slender, but persistent digging has shown that, even yet, many discoveries await the sieve and spade of the excavator'.[45] He could not have been more prophetic had he have known.

---

[44] Paul Pettitt *Secrets from the Crypt, Archaeology and Conservation in Derbyshire,* Issue 6, January 2009, p. 19
[45] *Palaeolithic Man in England: New Light on Age of the Cavemen, The Times,* 22nd December, 1924

6
Neanderthals and Moderns: the search for Creswell Man

'He had done as much as was possible for him. His large head, with the thick frontal bones, must have been very good for butting a brother Neanderthal, but it was no use against the stone wall of advancing civilisation, and like the Tasmanian and Bushman, the Red Indian and Australian of nowadays, he fades out of the picture, and his place is taken by a cleverer people'.

M & C.H.B. Quenell, *Everyday Life in the Old Stone Age* (1921)

In this chapter we will look more closely at the people who inhabited Creswell Crags in the Ice Age, the Neanderthals and the anatomically modern humans, or as Stringer and Gamble describe them 'the Ancients and the Moderns'.[1] There is a danger here that using this terminology segregates the two species by some great antiquated divide as the phrase alone conjures ideas that the Ancients (the Neanderthals) inhabited a world in the distant past and that the Moderns lived in, well, the modern. Therefore, we may adopt subconscious links with the Moderns for ourselves in the present, and this may be no great inaccuracy but, although there are differences (in appearance, actions and cognitive thought processes) the two species are not wholly dissimilar. After all, both species evolved from a common ancestor in Africa around 200-150,000 years ago. So let us start with the Neanderthals, the first inhabitants at Creswell Crags some 50-60,000 years ago and then compare them to the Moderns who first appeared around 45,000 years ago.

The quote above by the Quenells in 1921 epitomises the savage, unsophisticated, unintelligent view of the Neanderthals that for a long time stuck with us – indeed, to call someone a Neanderthal today is a derogatory term that implies a brutish, uncivilised manner. The typified 'cave man' image of a hairy brute wielding a club and sounding the word 'ug!' still reflects, for many, the Neanderthal persona. And yet work over the

---

[1] Stringer, C & Gamble, C *In Search of the Neanderthals,* (New York), 1993

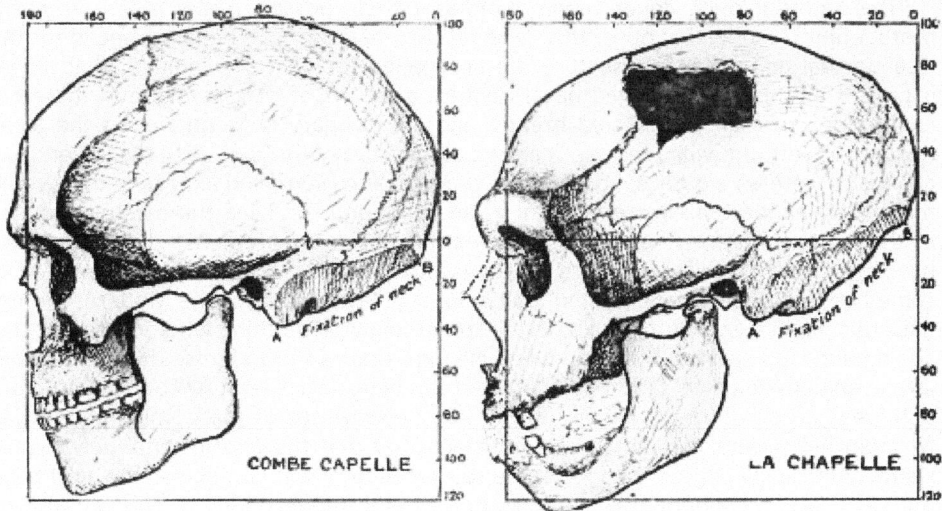

6.1 – *Skull comparison of a Neanderthal (La Chapelle) and Homo sapiens (Combe Capelle)* (Arthur Keith, 1915)

last thirty years or so has radically changed our view on our distant cousins. We would now stress that 'the Neanderthals were not ape-men, nor missing links – they were as human as us, but they represented a different brand of humanity, one with a distinctive blend of primitive and advanced characteristics'.[2] Indeed, the American anthropologists Coolidge and Wynn recently argued that the 'Neanderthals represented the zenith of a cognitive strategy that had evolved in Europe for several hundred thousand years... (they were) very successful, so much so that in the first encounter between Neanderthals and anatomically modern humans, Neanderthals prevailed. But 60,000 years later they lost out, largely, we contend, because of a small, but significant advantage carried in the modern human mind'.[3] We will return to this 'significant advantage' later for it may well hold the key to the subsequent rise of the Moderns and the demise of the Neanderthals, but for now we shall concentrate on the more physical attributes from within the archaeological record as they tell their own equally fascinating story.

Physically, Neanderthals and Moderns were different. From skeletal remains we know that Neanderthals were relatively short (about 5ft 6in for males) and stocky (around 80kg or 176lbs). They were heavily muscled, had a barrel-like trunk and had shorter lower limbs (forearms and lower legs) than their upper limbs. This is reflective of Bergmann's and Allen's rules relating to body proportion: 'cold adapted mammals have compact bodies (Bergmann) and shorter limbs (Allen) to maximize heat retention and reduce heat loss'.[4] Simply put, they were better adapted physically to surviving the cold than modern humans were and this point is extremely puzzling when we consider the adaptability-fate for the Neanderthals and is a point we shall return to subsequently. They also had marked differences in facial features, with the Neanderthal skull being much larger to house their larger brains (a factor which does not, however, imply greater intelligence) as well as both the brow ridges and nose being considerably more prominent than those of the Moderns.

---

[2] Ibid, p. 219
[3] Coolidge, F L & Wynn, T *The Rise of Homo Sapiens: the Evolution of Modern Thinking*, (Chichester), 2009
[4] see Coolidge & Wynn *The Rise of Homo Sapiens*, 2009, p. 182

The anthropologist Roger Lewin summarised the possible reasons for the more protuberant Neanderthal nose thus: 'several explanations have been advanced for the Neanderthal mid-facial architecture...an adaptation for warming inhaled frigid air as it passed through the enlarged nasal cavities; a means of condensing, and therefore conserving, moisture in exhaled breath; and a secondary consequence in the facial region of severe chewing pressures centred at the front of the jaw'.[5] So if the larger nasal capacities were an aid for controlling the temperature of inhaled air, surely that would make the Neanderthals more efficient at adapting and surviving the harsher climates of the Ice Age when compared to the Moderns? For example, inhaled cold air could have been warmed thus protecting the lungs and preventing illness such as pneumonia, something that would have proved fatal in Ice Age times, and yet the Moderns did not have this physical attribute. Again, this is something worth noting when contemplating adaptability and survival levels between Neanderthals and Moderns. There is another interesting physiological difference between the two species relating to bone structure and ideas on childbirth. From examining early discoveries of (predominantly partial) Neanderthal skeletal remains it was initially noted that the Neanderthal pelvic canal seemed unusually large, which led some to speculate that their babies may have been born at a later developmental stage (compared with modern births). This can also be noted in primate childbirth. However, in 1987 at the site of Kebara in Israel a more complete specimen was discovered, and from these remains it could be seen that it was not in fact the birth canal that was markedly different but the length of the pelvic bone itself. This anatomical difference between Neanderthal and Modern pelves 'supports the conclusion that Neanderthals represent a dead end in human evolution, not a stage on the way to *homo sapiens*'.[6] Here seemed to be conclusive proof that the Neanderthals were not a primitive 'stepping stone' from early hominids to fully modern humans, but rather an evolutionary brother (or sister!).

Let us now return to the idea of Neanderthal genetics and bodily composition. We have already noted that the limb-length ratios of Neanderthals suggests, based on Bergmann's and Allen's rules (see above), that they should have been able to adapt more easily than the Moderns and further work has been done on this issue by Erik Trinkaus at the University of Mexico. Trinkaus' work compared shin: thigh bone ratios (ie. tibia: femur) and by comparing different species he argued that it was possible to tell which climate they are best adapted to. Colder conditions, he believed, would require a more spherical body shape, whilst for hotter conditions a cylindrical shape would be needed. Now, we have already noted that Neanderthals were short and stocky (spherical) so their ideal climate would be a cold one, whereas modern humans were taller and less muscular (cylindrical) which denotes a warmer climatic preference. So, in theory, Neanderthals *should* have been more adapted to the depth of the last Ice Age than modern humans. We will look closely at manufacturing and technology shortly and see how this could have affected sustainability, but for now it will suffice to consider briefly an overall view based upon the archaeological remains left by the Neanderthals. Evidence of camps and long-term habitation is, on the whole, lacking as too is the use of hearths but many stone tools, animal bones and other evidence does survive. Indeed, Coolidge & Wynn suggest that ' the richness of Neanderthal archaeology ...reveals some of the features of (their) social world, and the resulting picture is one of small, local groups, who rarely if ever travelled beyond the confines of their own river valleys'.[7] This latter point is interesting as it is the same picture noted at Creswell – instead of travelling to obtain the technologically superior resource of flint for tool manufacture,

---

[5] Roger Lewin *Human Evolution: an illustrated introduction*, 3rd edition, (Cambridge, MA), 1993
[6] Ibid, p. 151
[7] Coolidge & Wynn *The Rise of Homo Sapiens,* 2009, p. 199

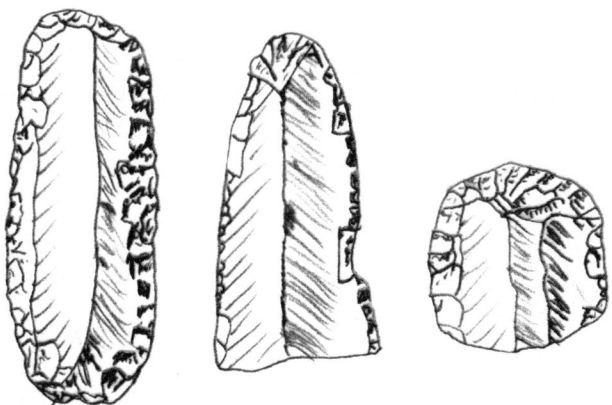

6.2 – *Châtelperronian blades from the type-site of Grotte des Fées*
(M. Beresford, redrawn from Gravina et al. 2005)

the Neanderthal inhabitants simply used the pebbles and cobbles obtained from the local river bed. This lifestyle choice is something that Clive Gamble terms a 'landscape of habit'.[8] However, one could argue that this is in itself evidence of expert procedural knowledge and attests to the Neanderthal's mastering their habitat and how to exploit it efficiently. By studying stone tool technology and how Neanderthals implemented this in relation to their locale we could argue that by using the quartzite that was available locally upon arrival at Creswell they adopted a much more energy- and time-efficient methodology. As Coolidge and Wynn point out 'one could respond to change by inventing something new, but this is something experts almost never do. It is quicker, and more reliable, to fall back on an alternative procedure. The more alternative procedures one can learn, hold in long-term memory, and have available, the better the response will be. This appears to be precisely the approach Neanderthals took to technology. Their corpus of procedural knowledge far exceeded that of *homo heidelbergensis* and may even have exceeded our own'.[9]

What we are looking at, both generally and specifically for our site at Creswell, is the Neanderthals 'staying put', that is, exploiting the local raw material rather than acquiring that best suited for the job at hand. That is not to say that quartzite did not make an effective tool, far from it, but flint as a natural resource is far superior. We should therefore note the wider social picture that this evidence is telling us, that the 'raw material evidence is actually quite important to our understanding. Neanderthal lives were local. They rarely travelled far from their home territories and had no long-range social networks on which they could rely'.[10] If this was the case, perhaps it is for this reason that the Neanderthals did not more fully utilise the varied resources for artefact production that we see the Moderns using, resources such as shell, amber, ivory and bone. Or perhaps there is some other explanation. To fully understand this we must combine two key areas, those of hunting and artefact association (whether through grave goods or artwork), and view them in relation to the factor hinted at earlier, Coolidge and Wynn's 'significant advantage'.

---

[8] Clive Gamble *The Palaeolithic Societies of Europe,* (Cambridge), 1986
[9] Coolidge & Wynn *The Rise of Homo Sapiens,* 2009, p. 196
[10] Ibid, p. 187

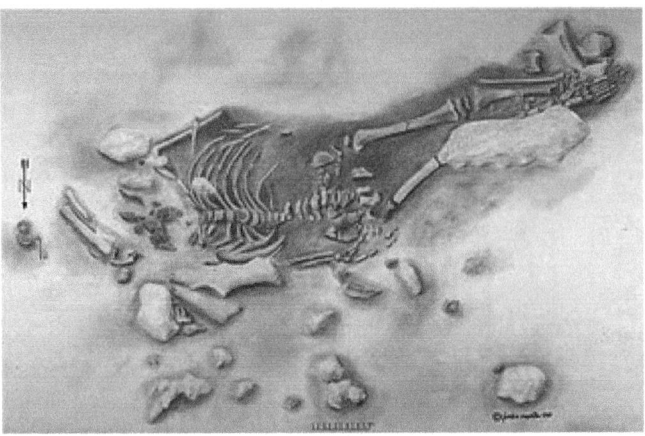

6.3 – *Child burial from Laghar Vello, Portugal*
(© Guida Casella)

This advantage relates to a theme that has featured heavily in the latter part of this work, that of cognitive thought processes. It is intended at this point to shed further light on exactly what this means in terms of our Neanderthal and Modern forebears. Before we look at hunting and what we can tell about society and the ability to plan and understand symbolic significances (both cognitive processes) through this, we must first briefly discuss exactly what happened when the Moderns arrived in the Neanderthal world. For western Europe there is evidence to suggest a period of around 10,000 years where both Neanderthals and Moderns co-existed. This does not mean they lived together, nor necessarily even got on, but they must surely have come into contact with each other fairly frequently. The debate continues as to whether the two species may have inter-bred and if clear evidence is discovered of this we may at least come to understand that there was some friendly interspersion between the two. There certainly is not any real evidence of hostilities or 'warfare' but then the skeletal remains are so few comparatively that again this is far from conclusive. There are suggestions of interbreeding however, notably the child from the site of Lagar Velho in Portugal (Lagar Velho 1 discovered in 1998). This discovery is rather controversial as the bones of the child appear to quite clearly reflect an admixture of both Neanderthal and Modern traits; the child is clearly a modern human as its mentum osseum development on the mandible (jaw) is a feature unique to Moderns, and yet many of the bones have Neanderthal characteristics, for example the femurs and the temporal bone. What is puzzling is that the date of the burial came out at 24,500BP which is a good five thousand years after the purposed Neanderthal extinction for western Europe. Although the grave inclusions and burial practices are clearly of a modern human nature, what is not clear is to why the skeletal remains are so anatomically distinct. Duarte et al believe that the morphological mosaic of the burial indicates that the 'child was not the result of a rare Neanderthal / early modern interbreeding but the descendant of extensively admixed populations'.[11] Does this therefore suggest a measure of co-existence between the two species then? This interaction, in whatever form and for whatever duration, is further supported by the lithic evidence of the stone tool assemblages known as the Châtelperronian culture. Generally, it is thought of as a regional industry in southwest France and Spain made by the final Neanderthal inhabitants of western Europe. A partial skeleton and skull from the site of Saint-Césaire in France of a Neanderthal was recovered from the higher of

---

[11] Duarte, C, Mauricio, J, Pettitt, P B, Souto, P, Trinkhaus, E, van der Plicht, H and Zilhao, J *The early Upper Palaeolithic human skeleton from the Abrigo do Lagar Velho (Portugal) and modern human emergence in Iberia, Proceedings of the National Academy of Sciences*, June 22, 1999, vol. 96, no. 13, pp.7604-09

two Châtelperronian levels and has been dated to c.36,000 years ago. However, it is the lithics themselves that are interesting as there are clear similarities between the Châtelperronian point or knife (featuring a curved back with blunting retouch) and the naturally backed knives of the Mousterian.[12] Although some scholars argue that these were local industries of a much wider Mousterian lithic technology, Stringer and Gamble believe instead they reflect a Neanderthal imitation of emerging Modern technologies. This belief mirrors those of the author already discussed that the Creswellian lithics are not a localised industry but rather an adaptive assemblage of a wider Magdalenian typology. So, if the Châtelperronian culture is Neanderthal we can note an extinction for the species in western Europe by c.31,000 years ago with the disappearance of this industry. Suddenly, the dates for the Lagar Velho child become increasingly interesting.

In terms of cognitive thought processes, then, the production of Châtelperronian blades makes for an interesting debate. Stringer and Gamble argue that 'the prepared core techniques that must have been used to produce them are a departure from both the (traditional) Levallois and disc core methods'.[13] As they further point out, producing a core that can be rotated to manufacture blades was an excellent innovation and was not strictly Upper Palaeolithic in technique, and although I would agree with them I would also argue that the archaeological record for Neanderthals does not reflect innovation and it can not be coincidence that their tool making repertoire should suddenly shift to this technique at just the same time as the Moderns arrived with a similar manufacturing methodology. Let us consider this point against the wider archaeological evidence. The Neanderthals had fire and yet they did not always cook their meat and there is certainly no evidence to suggest that the fires were lit in well-built hearths that would have been the foci for social activity (unlike the modern humans), they used wood for tools and weapons but did not use bone or antler and there is evidence at at least forty Neanderthal sites for the use of the manganese dioxide pigment and yet there is no evidence for art. These examples attest to a relatively low (compared to the Moderns) level of cognitive thought processes. Interestingly, this latter point regarding the manganese oxide may in fact relate to tool production, as Middle Stone Age sites in Africa often bear evidence that their inhabitants were mixing this pigment with sand and plant resins to make adhesives that could be used for hafting spears.[14]

Let us quickly consider burial practices in relation to cognitive thought processes and compare a late Neanderthal burial with the practices of the Moderns. We have already discussed the burial at Lagar Velho with its suggested Neanderthal links, but one burial definitely of a Neanderthal date yet reflecting Modern 'ritual' practices is that from the site of Shanidar, Iraq. Here an interred body was surrounded by pollen grains, which may give evidence that the body was covered in flower garlands prior to burial. Sceptics argue that the grains could just as easily be an accumulation of grains as the result of animal burrowing or percolation through the soils.[15] If the grains do represent the laying of flowers over the dead body what did they mean? Did the Neanderthals even know what it meant or were they simply copying an act that they had witnessed the modern humans doing? We shall probably never know, and yet it is interesting that the act of laying flowers at the graves of the dead is an act that has survived (from a modern human point of view) to this day. Perhaps with the discovery of more Neanderthal burials we may obtain a clearer picture in the future. Clive Gamble[16] has argued, however, that

---

[12] Stringer & Gamble *In Search of the Neanderthals,* 1993, p. 181
[13] Ibid, p. 200
[14] Coolidge & Wynn *The Rise of Homo Sapiens,* 2009, p. 191-92
[15] Stringer & Gamble *In Search of the Neanderthals,* 1993, p. 158
[16] Gamble, C *Grave shortcomings; the evidence for Neanderthal burial,* in Current Anthropology, 30, 1989, pp. 181-82

Neanderthal burials only really survive in more-or-less complete state in areas where carnivore evidence is slight, for example in caves where only a small number of carnivore remains have been present. For Creswell, given the high carnivore occupation levels, the chances of any Neanderthal remains having survived antiquity were remote indeed, and of the known skeletal remains from the caves there none are deemed to be Neanderthal.

One interesting piece of evidence from a modern human perspective (and could possibly relate to human remains from the Creswell caves and the Cheddar Gorge discussed in Chapter 5) is that from the Ethiopian site of Herto, c.160,000 years ago. Here, three skulls bore evidence of post-mortem 'damage' – one had been defleshed with a stone tool and all three had 'polished' surfaces that may suggest they had been carried in a bag.[17] Just as was argued in the previous chapter this does not need reflect cannibalism or head cults, but is good early evidence that modern humans related heads or skulls to power, spiritualism or ritual. As we are dealing with such a remote period of our history much of our theories will perhaps never be more than educated guesswork or theories but one thing that is for certain regarding our 'transitional' period is that the Neanderthals became extinct and we Moderns survived. Again, there is a debate as to why this occurred – was it hostility between the two species, a poorer adaptability rate for Neanderthals in light of worsening climatic conditions or a combination of the two – but it is worth noting as to just how subtle it may have been, and yet once it began could have quickly led to extinction. Regardless of the actual cause, 'a subsistence advantage of just one per cent by modern humans in competition with Neanderthals, for instance, could result in complete replacement within 30 generations, or a millenium'.[18] Even more precise was Ezra Zubrow's 'trail of death' theory that showed, through a computer-simulated model, how a Neanderthal mortality rate (perhaps caused by increased stress or poorer living conditions in the fringe lands) of just two per cent higher than that of the modern humans could have easily led to extinction in just 1,000 years.[19]

The most striking difference between the Neanderthals and the Moderns is consciousness and there is nothing better to reflect this than symbology. The two key areas, hunting and art (in various forms) link nicely in with this concept

6.4 – *The Lowenmensch carving from Hohlenstein-Stadel*
(Public Domain)

---

[17] Coolidge & Wynn *The Rise of Homo Sapiens*, 2009, p. 209
[18] Lewin *Human Evolution*, 1993, p. 151
[19] Zubrow, E *The Demographic Modelling of Neanderthal Extinction* in Mellars, P & Stringer, C (eds) *The Human Revolution: Behavioural and Biological Perspectives on the Origins of Modern Humans*, (Edinburgh), 1989, pp. 212-31

and I would argue are inter-linked themselves. I have already discussed in detail the artwork from Creswell and its possible links with hunting and animal representation / spiritualism in chapter three but it is worth going back to this in relation to consciousness and cognition in a Neanderthal vs Modern approach. I wish to begin the hunting / art discussion by considering the small, mammoth ivory carving from Hohlenstein-Stadel. Approximately 30cm (12 inches) in height and dating to c.32,000 years ago, the carving represents a 'Löwenmensch' (Lion Man) in that it is half-man, half lion. The concept of this *art mobilier* is fascinating in itself as to take a 'classified' organism (in this case a lion) and combine it with a different 'category' organism (ie. a human) is a clear indicator of analogical reasonings and therefore enhanced working memory. As Coolidge and Wynn agree 'it is not the image but the *abstract concept* (author's emphasis) behind it that argues for modern executive functions and working memory'.[20] Is it not, therefore, neither lion nor human but a representative combination of both? Perhaps this links back to the concept of shamanism discussed earlier in relation to cave paintings and engravings. It is becoming clearer with the increased number of known sites that Palaeolithic 'wall art is mainly of large mammals – bison, aurochs, deer, horses, mammoth, ibex and so on – but carnivores are rare...images are often very good, naturalistic representations of single animals, or small groups of individuals but there is little sense of natural scenes'.[21] It is almost as if the artist is the hunter, and the subject the prey. Put another way, the animals depicted on the cave walls are representations of animals that are to become prey to the hunter / artist. This 'hunter / artist' theory is further supported if we consider body ornamentation (something I would argue is in many ways a continuation of artistry) ie. jewellery. Carnivore teeth are usually represented in very high proportions. Is this the hunter seeking to turn himself into the deadly carnivore in order to aid in the hunting process? Suddenly, a great deal of light is shed onto our Lion-man carving. And again this has serious connotations for the shamanism theory adopted by many for the creation of art on cave walls and may in some ways represent an idea of shape-shifting (think of the 'sorcerer' from Les Troires Freres).

On this train of thought, we could question why art disappears with the end of the last Ice Age. Was it because art had some link to the landscape and hunting methods, factors that altered radically once the ice had gone and the landscape was altered irrevocably? When it later returns in the Neolithic (c.4000-1800BC) and Bronze Ages (c.1800-700BC) it is quite stylistic with geometric patterning becoming the main characteristic, and from this we could suggest that it is by then mainly aesthetic. Whatever the reason behind Palaeolithic art, it can not surely be merely the 'art for art's sake' theory as was first thought (and has fairly recently been revived)? John Halverson of the University of California believed that the art is a product 'not of "primitive mind" but "primal mind", human consciousness in the process of growth'.[22] I would disagree, particularly when considering the female engravings from the Church Hole or the engraved horse rib bone from Robin Hood Cave at Creswell. Equally interesting at Creswell is Boyd Dawkins' excavation diary for Church Hole, in which he mentions the presence of red ochre.[23] Perhaps this was used for painting in the cave in a (potentially) similar manner to the manganese oxide (see chapter 3)? It could equally have been used in body adornment or perhaps as a preservative for skins. We will probably never know, much along the same lines as we may never know the true purpose of the Palaeolithic art. As Margaret Conkey

---

[20] Coolidge & Wynn *The Rise of Homo Sapiens*, 2009, p. 232-33
[21] Lewin *Human Evolution*, 1993, p. 183
[22] Halverson, J *Art for art's sake in the Palaeolithic*, in *Current Anthropology*, vol. 28, 1987, pp. 63-89
[23] see Pettitt & Jacobi *The Palaeolithic archaeology of Creswell Crags*, in Bahn, P & Pettitt, P *Britain's Oldest Art*, (Swindon), 2009, pp. 16-35

rather poignantly suggested, 'perhaps we have closed off certain lines of inquiry simply by using the label "art"'.[24]

Further evidence is provided into the levels of human consciousness when we study Late Upper Palaeolithic hunting practices. Generally we see Neanderthals hunting 'close-up, that is getting in close to an animal and using brute strength and close-range thrusting actions with flint-tipped spears to kill prey. As Coolidge and Wynn explain 'injury patterns on Neanderthals themselves attest to close-in killing. Healed upper-body and head injuries are common on Neanderthal skeletons, and the kinds of injuries mimic those received today by rodeo athletes'.[25] Perhaps this reflects a certain degree of opportunistic, 'aggressive' hunting practices? Stringer and Gamble argue that there are certain necessities for successful hunting strategies, in that 'a fully planned hunting strategy depends on far-flung social contacts'.[26] These would allow for much-needed requirements such as being able to obtain food in times of hardships, providing 'marriage' partners and binding people together over distance by widespread 'systems of alliance' – 'these networks of exchange, therefore, are part of a much wider survival strategy (that is) essential in a harsh environment'.[27] This is certainly true of the modern humans with their widespread social and trade networks attested to by the archaeological record, but what of the Neanderthals? There is a debate as to how much was hunted and how much was scavenged but as Stringer and Gamble argue *both* of these methods require a good degree of planning: 'both hunting and scavenging involve making decisions about where to move in the landscape in order to stand the best chance of intercepting game, dead or alive'.[28]

There is good archaeological evidence to show that Neanderthals did use both of these methods if circumstances required it, which to my mind suggests the ability to forward plan and make *a certain amount* of cognitive decisions. The anthropologist M C Stiner[29] found that at the cave site of Guattari at Monte Circeo in Italy there were two distinct faunal stratigraphies. The upper layers (levels 1 and 2) had gnawed animal bones and many skulls indicative of hyaena denning with little evidence of human use. The lower layers (levels 3 and 4) had bones with fewer gnaw marks and very little in terms of skeletal remains of hyaena – clearly not a den. Curiously, the layers were still dominated by skulls, which most likely reflects a scavenging method adopted by the Neanderthals very similar to that of the hyaenas. Kuhn, however, found at the site of Grotta di Sant' Agostino near Gaeta in Italy that the bones there reflected much clearer hunting practices. Both red and fallow deer were present and the bones showed that they had been hunted as most of the carcass was represented in the skeletal assemblage and cut marks outnumbered gnaw marks.[30] These examples show that Neanderthals used whatever methods were needed and that they 'pursued a goal of subsistence security and met this with a range of behavioural solutions'.[31] Stiner asked the question as to why Neanderthals were scavenging the heads of carcasses at the Grotta Guattari, after all they would have been relatively void of meat so they must have been targeting them for some other reason. Stiner believes it was probably the fat reserves that were

---

[24] quoted in Lewin *Human Evolution*, 1993, p. 186
[25] Coolidge & Wynn *The Rise of Homo Sapiens*, 2009, p. 184
[26] Stringer & Gamble *In Search of the Neanderthals*, 1993, p. 164
[27] Ibid. p. 165
[28] Ibid. p. 164
[29] Stiner, M C *The faunal remains at Grotta Guattari: a taphonomic perspective*, Current Anthropology, 32 (2), 1991, pp. 103-17
[30] Kuhn, S. L. *"Unpacking" reduction: lithic raw material economy in the Mousterian of West-Central Italy*, Journal of Anthropological Archaeology, 10, 1991, pp. 76-106
[31] Stringer & Gamble *In Search of the Neanderthals*, 1993, p. 166

retained in the skull that the Neanderthals were after, perhaps reflecting a scarcity of nutrition in the lean winter months, reserves that may have been particularly important to pregnant females or children.

Research at Harvard University recently studied the dental remains of horse (which grow continually to recover from use) in order to obtain a clearer picture on Neanderthal and Modern hunting practices. Darker layers in the teeth reflect winter growth when nutrition is low, whilst lighter layers reflect spring / summer grazing. The team at Harvard studied the final layer of growth as this would have reflected growth just prior to death and human consumption. Interestingly, horse remains from Neanderthal sites had a more-or less equal share of dark and light 'final growth' layers, whilst Modern sites had *either* dark or light layers. This seems to suggest, then, a prolonged Neanderthal occupation for the sites compared to a more mobile and sporadic modern human existence, and this fits in with the general theories discussed that the Moderns were more 'mobile' hunters whilst the Neanderthals preferred to 'stay put' and hunt in whatever method was needed. This argument does, however, have its weaknesses as if a co-existence in one area meant a duality in terms of game exploitation, and the modern humans moved on leaving a 'poor crop' for the Neanderthals (ie. the few animals that had not been killed or moved on) surely, faced with starvation and ultimately extinction would the Neanderthals not simply move on too? No matter how set in their ways they may have been, it beggars belief that they would not have altered their 'traditional' practices just to remain in their comfort zone when faced with certain hardships, particularly when they could quite clearly see what the Moderns were doing (and we know they emulated them in other ways so why not in hunting practice?). Its not as if the Neanderthals do not have a history of nomadic movement, and they certainly adapted well enough when faced with harsher climates in the past – remember the scene from Robin Hood Cave where the archaeology reflected a Neanderthal retreat with the coming of the extreme ice only to return once the weather had warmed up. Also, if the Moderns were exploiting game in 'Neanderthal territory', so much so that it was making it difficult for the Neanderthals to feed themselves, would this not have inevitably led to conflict? And yet there is no evidence for this.

Let us now focus in on the modern humans' hunting practices and attempt to understand why they were technologically better, for surely they must have been in the end as they survived and the Neanderthals did not? As far back as 1981, Richard Leakey had realised the connection between the landscape and the methods of hunting that were used in that locale. As he pointed out 'it is interesting that many living sites are unsuitable locations for generalised, opportunistic hunting but are superbly strategic for the manipulation and possible corralling of herds'.[32] Creswell certainly fits that notion, its long, narrow valley being an ideal 'gateway' through the higher ground to either side into which prey could be driven into waiting ambushes or chased over the cliff tops. A similar site is that of La Vache on the Vicdessos River near Ariège, located as it is in the 'bottleneck' of the valley. Here, around eighty-five percent of the large mammal remains uncovered were of ibex and dated to around 13,000 years ago (again, a very similar age to the height of modern human occupation at Creswell). It is obvious from this extremely high proportion that the ibex were purposefully targeted and exploited. Paul Bahn believes that 'a single hunter attempting to pick off animals in gregarious groups usually has little luck, and the herd is inevitably disturbed...the Palaeolithic people may have exploited the tendency of ibex to go uphill when driven, directing a small group from the main herd towards concealed hunters'.[33] Suddenly, the caves at Creswell appear more useful than for merely sleeping in.

---

[32] Richard Leakey *The Making of Mankind*, 1981, p. 187
[33] quoted in Leakey, *Making of Mankind*, p. 189

So it appears that modern humans did not use opportunistic hunting but rather 'managed hunting'. Paul Bahn's comment about leading a small group away from the herd into a waiting ambush is interesting, and if we consider the engraving of the horse from Robin Hood Cave at Creswell it may reflect similar practices. If we look carefully at the engraving it is possible to note a series of vertical lines drawn over the top of the horse itself. Jill Cook of the British Museum discussed her ideas that these lines may represent 'guide posts' placed in the ground to lure the galloping horse into a waiting ambush.[34] She commented how modern reindeer hunters use similar methods as the animals see the wooden posts out of the corner of their eye as they are running and believe it to be a solid fence, so instead of simply running through the gaps between the guide posts and escaping they continue to follow the marked out path. Could this be what the lines on the horse engraving represent, as the engraved horse is almost certainly galloping at speed in the artwork? Perhaps this sheds further light onto the artefact, as it could be designed to show others how the people at Creswell hunted, or perhaps it was some offering to a hunting God or designed to give power to the hunters? Archaeological remains show a similar exploitation to La Vache (interestingly this time with horse) at the French site of Solutré and the British site of Cheddar Gorge in Somerset.

There is a final piece of evidence that relates to the use of horse that is worth discussing at this point and that is the number of so-called *bâton de commandements* found on many sites across Europe. We are still uncertain as to what these objects were used for, but they originally got their name as they were assumed to belong to 'chiefs' or 'leaders' who would wear them around their neck or waist, almost as power symbols. They would be suspended, it was thought, by tying a piece of twine, rope or leather through the hole drilled in one end (analysis has shown that generally the hole has an 'hour-glass' shape, meaning the hole was drilled from one side halfway through before the object was turned over and the hole completed from the other side) and then tying this around the body. Other suggestions are that they could instead have been arrow straighteners, with the shaft of the arrow being inserted into the drilled hole and then bent against the artefact in order to straighten the shaft. Boyd Dawkins discussed this in his book *Cave Hunting* in relation to the Eskimos and a specific example of an Eskimo arrow staightener held in the British Museum. He stated that 'if it (the British Museum example) be compared with the so-called "bâton de commandement" it will be seen, that the latter also was probably intended for the same purpose; the difference in the shape of the hole being also observable in the series of Eskimos arrow-straighteners in the British Museum, and being largely due to friction by use'.[35]

Yet further suggestions are that they could be part of some sort of pulley system, perhaps as part of a horse harness. Tooth wear on some horse remains does suggest they may have had a bit in their mouth but this is still uncertain. However, one rather interesting theory relates to modern day Inuits as they use similar artefacts to feed the reins of their sleds through and then hold them in the hand in order to guide the animal pulling the sled. This avoids the reins themselves having to be held thus preventing burns but also means that by pulling on the implement the driver could easily turn the sled at speed.

Modern Creswell Man could well have used the gorge for managed hunting 'on site' (although at this late stage exploitation of arctic hare was most common, as we have seen) as well as simply camping there, but there are a few other sites in the region that offer more information on this. These sites make up the Creswell Heritage Area, but

---

[34] pers. comm. Jill Cook to the author, July 2009
[35] William Boyd Dawkins *Cave Hunting*, 1874, p. 355

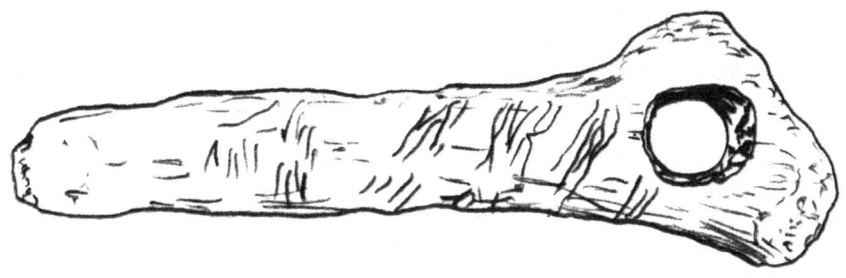

6.5 – *A bâton-de-commandement found at Gough's Cave, Cheddar Gorge*
(M. Beresford, redrawn from Wymer, 1984)

6.6 – *Inuit arrow straightener*
(Boyd Dawkins, 1874)

although the majority of the cave sites held Ice Age archaeology, only a couple had signs of human occupation and I would now like to focus on two of these sites, those of Ash Tree Cave, Whitwell and Langwith Bassett Cave at Langwith. Alan Leslie Armstrong did much of the work at Ash Tree Cave in the late 1940s and early 1950s. The cave itself is located in a shallow valley known locally as Burntfield Grips and comprises a short passage that leads to a small inner chamber. Armstrong began his excavations in 1949 and part of the archaeological deposits he found there were human remains. Within the inner chamber a pile of stones had been placed over a collection of human remains that comprised two individuals, one of which was a male aged 18-20. Much of the skeleton had been preserved but no pelvic bone, skull or mandible was present. Although the skeleton later turned out, through radiocarbon dating, to be of a Neolithic age, I find it interesting that the skull and jaw were missing, as this bears some similarities to the remains from Creswell, albeit here the skull (or fragments of) tended to be present, nevertheless there could be some connection.

To the right of this first deposit of bones, six inches lower down, a second collection was found. This time, a clavicle, several phalanges and vertebra, a mandible of 'exceptionally robust type' and the mandible of an infant were present. Armstrong assures us that these remains were not part of the first collection.[36] There was also present an adult mandible that was quite primitive, particularly in the width of the ascending ramus, the shallowness of the sigmoid notch and its general robustness. It also had abnormal dentition – it had only three incisors instead of four. Professor R. W. Lovel of King's College, Newcastle believed the missing tooth to be a central one and that it had been

---

[36] A. L. Armstrong *28th Interim report of the Committee for the exploration of Caves in the Derbyshire district*, Report to the British Association, Section H, Anthropology, 1956, (unpublished)

lost in early life, as only three sockets remained.[37] Beyond the area with the burials the cave appeared to terminate but excavation revealed a rear passage that contained a cist with the remains of two further individuals. Amongst these was another mandible with signs of distortion, probably due to severe osteoarthritis.[38] As these remains were at the back of the cave they must have predated the other burials but no pottery or grave goods were recovered with any of the burials, although all burial locations had evidence of charcoal and flint flakes.

The cave also had an earlier 'Creswellian' (Magdalenian) layer with evidence of wood, ash and charcoal (ie. fires) and flints of Creswellian type. Also, three microliths (presumably Mesolithic) were recovered very similar to those from Whaley Shelter No. 2. The overall belief was that Ash Tree Cave was used as a casual, sporadic camp site much like the caves at Creswell, but probably on a much more infrequent level. There was also evidence for Neanderthal use of the cave, with Mousterian 'Zone 3' apparently containing several bone awls and two bird tibias that were perforated at one end and were initially thought by Armstrong to be decorative ornaments or amulets.[39] Whilst I do not doubt that these artefacts were indeed recovered from the site, Armstrong must have been incorrect in attributing these to Neanderthal levels and they are almost certainly of a Late Upper Palaeolithic date. In his 2nd report from the site, Armstrong mentioned a hearth was uncovered and that this was situated over a fissure approximately 18inches wide in the rock floor. A Mousterian side scraper was recovered at a depth of 12inches and a reindeer antler awl was found beside the hearth.[40]

The cave site of Langwith Bassett within the Creswell Heritage Area is also of interest as it too harboured evidence of Creswellian use and of human remains. Much of the work done at Langwith was by the Rev. Edwin Mullins in the early 20th century, but his story goes back several years prior to this. Mullins first visited the cave in the winter of 1870-71 and was told that it was 'commonly believed that a subterranean passage existed formerly between the old church on the south side of the valley of the Poulter... and a farmhouse on the opposite (side)'.[41] Local tales told of youngsters that managed to find this 'passage' and gain entrance to it by crawling through a gap (it had allegedly been bricked up to keep foxes from going to earth by request of the Rufford Hunt) and others that suggested local poachers used to hide their spoil there.[42] In 1896 Mullins became Rector at Langwith and carried out 'careful investigations' to try and locate the passage, but to no avail.

Several years later his children told him they had found it – at the top of the valley, not in the bottom where his previous efforts had focussed, hidden behind some nettles and brambles. There he found an archway some 2ft high and 3ft wide, and upon entering this he found a cave. On September 17th 1903 his children cleared away some earth and small stones at the back of this cave and found an inner chamber with a scattering of bones, resulting in Mullins deciding to apply for permission to explore the cave properly to the owner of the land, the Duke of Devonshire, and in the Christmas holidays of 1903 they set to work. The front of the cave was cleared to the natural floor level but only traces of fire and a few flints were discovered. On the left-hand side of the cave, however, there was a 'natural arch' that Mullins thought was most likely created by a partial roof

---

[37] Ibid. p. 1
[38] Ibid. p. 2
[39] Ibid. p. 2
[40] A. L. Armstrong *29th Interim report of the Committee for the exploration of Caves in the Derbyshire district*, Report to the British Association, Section H, Anthropology, 1957, (unpublished)
[41] Rev. E.H. Mullins *Langwith Cave, Transactions of the East Derbyshire Field Club*, 1907, p. 32
[42] Ibid. p. 32

collapse.[43] Under this, approximately 2ft down, a human skull was discovered, although the jaw was missing. From his work in the cave, Mullins believed that it was 'easy to picture prehistoric man with his fire at his feet singing Dulce Domum, after a long hunt for food for his family upon snow clad earth without, with only his flint flakes to help him in the chase'.[44]

In his report of the work carried out Mullins explains that the 'arch' was constructed of five or six stones resting between the cave wall and a larger stone. He deemed it natural and commented that 'it appeared like a fall of roof, but no sign was visible of the spot whence it had fallen'.[45] It is interesting how the description of this 'arch' is similar to the structures noted at Ash Tree Cave and may well have been some form of burial structure. Traces of fire were noted beneath it. The skull itself was examined by Professor Keith at the Royal College of Surgeons and he noted how the facial part had been broken away and was missing along with the jaw, although the part that remained was quite well preserved. The cranial features were those of a male with the sutures reflecting an age of between 45-55.[46] Keith further commented that the Langwith skull was typical of Professor Huxley's 'River-bed' skulls and was comparable to those from Muskham, Nottinghamshire and Towyn-y-capel in Wales. Huxley believed these 'River-bed' people inhabited the Late Palaeolithic and Early Neolithic, as at this point the Mesolithic was not yet recognised. As we saw in chapter five, radiocarbon dating for the Langwith skull actually places it quite firmly in the Iron Age which means Professor Keith was mistaken in his attributing it to the River-bed model.

After this initial exploration, work was halted due to the outbreak of war as was explained in an article in the *Transactions of the East Derbyshire Field Club*, who paid a visit to Langwith Cave in 1918:

> *'exploration had been suspended since just before the outbreak of war, and the interior, it was thought, might need some expert attention before it was in a fit condition to receive, with perfect safety, so large a party'.*[47]

In 1927 work was resumed at Langwith by Alan Leslie Armstrong and Dorothy Garrod as part of the British Association's cave exploration programme. Armstrong reported that 'a reconnaissance of Langwith Cave indicates that only a portion of that cave has been fully explored. Permission has been obtained to complete this and it is hoped to undertake it in the autumn'.[48] Garrod excavated the northern passage and found a similar stratigraphy to that of Mullins. Pleistocene bones were present throughout the cave and included woolly rhinocerous, reindeer and hyaena. Notable Palaeolithic flints included Mousterian tools (Mullins), Upper Aurignacian flints (Garrod) and Creswellian tools (Mullins) including a Cheddar point found just inside the entrance to the cave, a Creswell point and an interesting tool that is an end scraper on one end and a burin on the other. So it would seem that, just as at Ash Tree Cave, our Creswell Man was using Langwith Bassett cave as an outlier within a hunting ground in the Creswell area, the main (seasonal) camp being in the Creswell caves themselves. And once again we appear

---

[43] Ibid. p. 34
[44] Ibid. p. 34. Dulce Domum refers here to a song written by Robert S. Ambrose in 1876. Its translation literally means 'Sweetly at home'
[45] Rev. E.H. Mullins *The Ossiferous Cave at Langwith, The Derbyshire Archaeological and Natural History Journal*, Vol. 35, 1913, p. 143
[46] Prof. Keith's report is included in Mullins *Ossiferous Cave*, 1913 p. 155-157
[47] 'A Visit to Langwith' in *Transactions of the East Derbyshire Field Club*, 1918, pp. 2-3
[48] Armstrong, A.L. *3rd Interim Report of the Committee for the exploration of Caves in the Derbyshire district, Report of the British Association for the Advancement of Science*, July 1924

92 Beyond the Ice

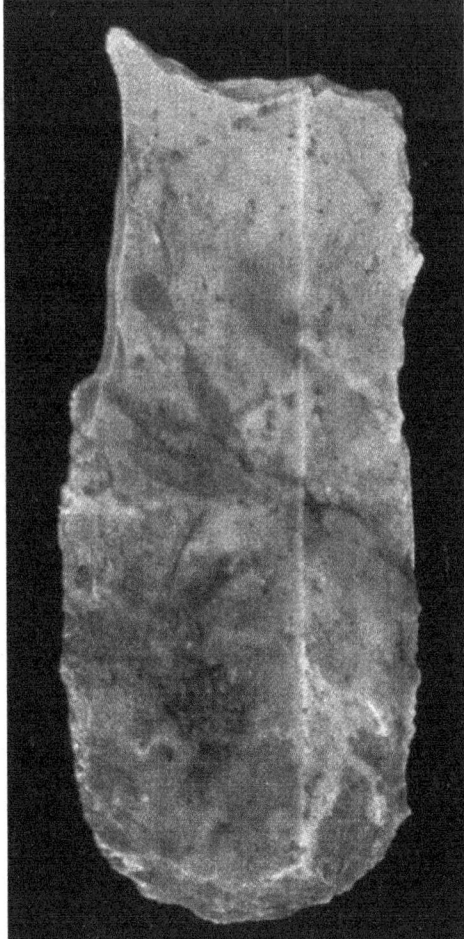

6.7 – End scraper / burin from Langwith
Bassett Cave
(© Creswell Heritage Trust)

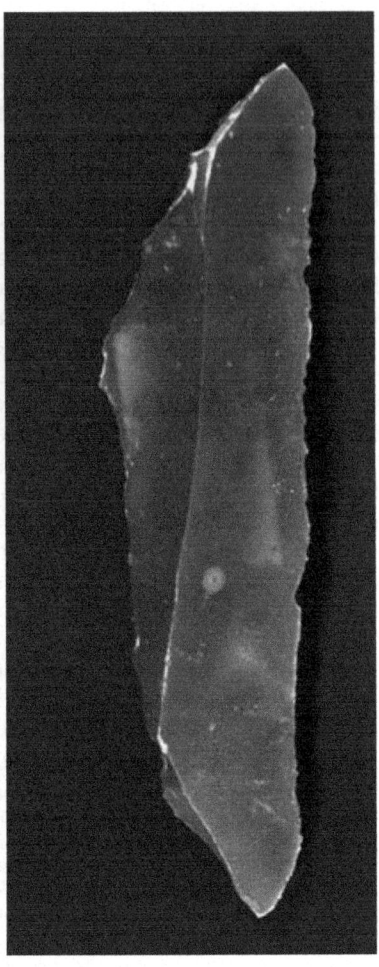

6.8 – Cheddar point from
Langwith Bassett Cave
(© Creswell Heritage Trust)

to have the indication that what at first glance could have potentially been Palaeolithic human remains, were in fact much later, as seems to be the case at Creswell.

The end of the Ice Age brought about major changes for Britain in its landscape, settlement and land use but, perhaps most importantly, it became an island and was finally cut off from mainland Europe, as it has stayed for the past ten thousand years. So what happened to our Creswell man? Pioneering new research is beginning to show that rather than being a fully-fledged prehistoric landscape, Britain may actually have been a mere fringe-land on the edge of a very different landscape than has so far been envisaged, a landscape that could well hold the key to what happened beyond the ice.

7

Final Remarks

'One looked forward to the day when the Palaeolithic would be presented as something other than a descriptive synthesis of archaeologically recovered things'

Lewis Binford, 1986, commenting on Clive Gamble's book *The Palaeolithic Settlement of Europe*.

These comments were made in praise for Clive Gamble's seminal work published in the mid-1980s, the point being that this book was seen as the foundations for an emerging understanding of a period that was, to most, the lost period of history. That is not to say that much important work was not carried out before this, far from it, but Gamble's work in many ways marked a turning point in Palaeolithic archaeology. It represented 'the day' that Binford alluded to in his quote above, and yet the times that Creswell Crags is mentioned in it can be counted on one hand, and this merely in passing. The aim of this book is to show that not only has this now changed thanks to the last twenty-five years of meticulous effort, but the importance of the site has surpassed any of our wildest expectations. Who would have believed that cave art existed in Britain? And who would have thought that the site would be worthy of close to £5m being spent on a visitor and interpretation centre? In the past, so little was understood of the importance of the site that a main road and a sewage works were constructed at its heart, as we have seen. Over the last six chapters, one hundred and forty years worth of investigation has been discussed and the height of our current knowledge expressed. But the story does not end there, in fact in many ways it is just beginning.

Recent research by a team from Birmingham University is beginning to reveal that, rather than being the land bridge that we for so long believed it to be, Doggerland may well in fact have been an entire continent in its own right, and could hold the key to our understanding of migratory patterns, settlement and landscape use. This past view is summed up by Gaffney, Fitch and Smith when they suggest that at the turn of the twentieth century 'the lack of substantive knowledge concerning this distant past confined lecturers and publications to little more than long and detailed descriptions of antler, bone or stone tools. There was only the vaguest idea of the age of the artefacts studied, whilst the societies that produced these tools left no histories to testify to their original use or significance.'[1] The past hundred years of scientific study have told us much about the environment, the climate and the landscape. For instance, we now know that at the end of the Pleistocene, melting north European ice sheets released 32million km³ of meltwater resulting in sea levels rising by around 83m (272ft), and between 18,000-5,500BC sea levels had risen by more than 140m. But although this aided our understanding of the people and how they lived considerably, it never quite revealed the whole picture. That is until 2001, when the team at Birmingham University began a project to use seismic data obtained from gas and oil companies in an attempt to extrapolate information about Doggerland. They were never sure whether their ideas would work. They did, and the results are revolutionary.

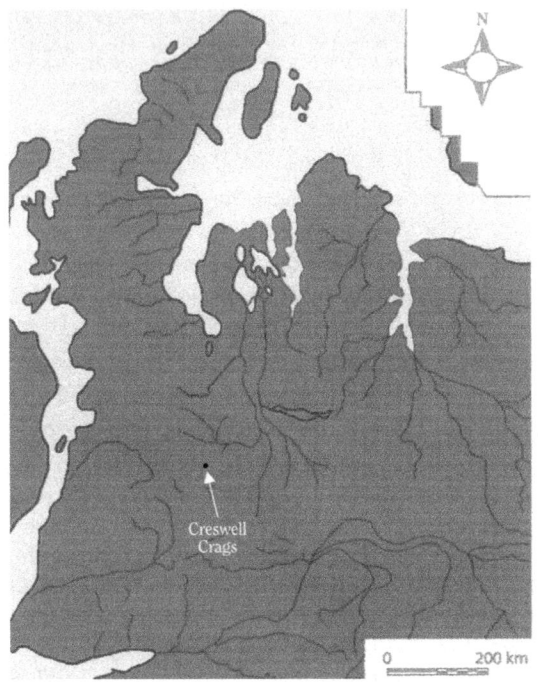

7.1 - *Map of Doggerland showing land mass before sea levels rose*
(© David Astbury. Rivers after Coles and Rouillard)

Petroleum Geo-Services gave the team access to 6000km² of seismic survey data and incredibly after just one month of study a computer-generated image clearly reflected a large river running across the Dogger Bank.[2] This river was almost as large as the Rhine and could be followed for 40km across the bank. 'The excitement amongst archaeologists following the discovery of this single river channel is possibly difficult to understand for anyone not actually an archaeologist' commented the team. Generally we knew that the barriers to occupation were the ice sheets, quite obviously, of Scandinavia and Northern Britain. What we did not know was what actually went on in between these areas. The team at Birmingham were going on the hypothesis that it was the availability of fuel for fires that was the key to a lack of settlement / land use rather than the cold climate: 'in Siberia lack of kindling and other fuels was a primary factor limiting settlement rather than the low temperatures.'[3] This outlook is interesting but makes perfect sense. The Younger Dryas period (11,000 - 9,600BC) saw a major cooling event which most likely made settlement quite sparse, or so the team believed. This meant that people at the

---

[1] Gaffney, v, Fitch, S & Smith, O Europe's Lost World: The rediscovery of Doggerland, (BA Research Report No. 160, (York), 2009

[2] Ibid. p. 34
[3] Ibid. p. 44

time would have needed to inhabit resource-rich environments that could sustain them in times of hardship. 'Doggerland was clearly a massive plain dominated by water: rivers, marshes and coastlines. To the contemporary eye this environment might have appeared featureless and even unattractive, yet, to Mesolithic communities, Doggerland was a rich environment and provided a wealth of opportunities'.[4] As they further argued 'the southern North Sea hides one of the most extensive, well-preserved early Holocene landscapes surviving in Europe. Despite this (it remains) one of the most enigmatic archaeological landscapes in the world.'

So far, twenty-four lakes or areas of wetland and around 1600km of river systems have been recorded. These would have undoubtedly provided the navigational routes into Britain that have been discussed already. However, rising sea levels at the time would have rapidly eroded the hospitable areas and created an ever-changing landscape -loss of coastal areas and fishing grounds for example. This in turn could have led to hostile altercations. Take the site at Skateholm in Sweden. Mithen[5] suggests the cemetery site there, which contained sixty-four burials, held evidence of violence. Four had depressed skull fractures, whilst another two had injuries resulting from being hit by arrows. This appears to suggest an altercation of some form, perhaps over land, as Skateholm 'must have been highly desirable for hunter-gatherers, with abundant supplies of food in the woodland, the marshes, the rivers, the lagoon and the sea. When the people dispersed in the summer they would not have wished to relinquish the lagoon to unexpected strangers, or to those who lived in adjacent but less productive regions.'[6] So if this is evidence of violence between Mesolithic communities who were attempting to survive in rapidly declining environments, should we not expect a similar picture for our Neanderthals and Modern Humans some 30,000 years earlier? For these 'invaders' were not only another group of hunter-gatherers to our Neanderthals, but another species entirely.

The Mesolithic period that occurred after the ice had retreated for the final time appears to have been just as volatile as the period preceding it. However, there appears to be a period of around two thousand years of our story missing. What exactly happened between the period around 12,500-10,500 years ago? In other words, what happened to our Creswell man before his Mesolithic cousins arrived? Once again, we can turn to local sites in order to provide a picture of this, but first we must look a little further afield. In the 2009 edition of Proceedings of the Prehistoric Society Chantal Conneller published her report on the Final Palaeolithic site of Rookery Farm, Cambridgeshire. Here, three 'penknife points' gave the site a date of around 12-11,000BP, whilst the debitage of the site reflected the use of a hard hammer, which could narrow this date down even further to between 11,500-11,000 BP based on continental industries. As Conneller explains 'flakes and blades were detached using a hard hammer. Bulbs (of percussion) are generally large with pronounced cones and bulbar scars, indicating that this was the habitual knapping method,'[7] whereas blade technology (ie. Creswell and Cheddar Points) normally involves the use of a soft hammer or punch. Also, the use of a single striking platform (as is generally the case in Late Upper Palaeolithic industries) produces curved blades[8] although blades from Rookery Farm curve less than traditional

---

[4] Ibid. p. 99
[5] Steve Mithen After the Ice, 2003
[6] Ibid. p. 175
[7] Conneller, C Investigation of a Final Palaeolithic site at Rookery Farm, Great Wilbraham, Cambridgeshire, in Proceedings of the Prehistoric Society, vol. 75, 2009, p. 175
[8] Jacobi, R A collection of Early Upper Palaeolithic artefacts from Beedings, near Pulborough, West Sussex, and the context of similar finds from the British Isles, in Proceedings of the Prehistoric Society, Vol. 73, 2007, pp.71-111

Creswellian lithics.[9] 'Assemblages containing penknife points belong to a separate chronological phase of the British later Upper Palaeolithic from assemblages containing Cheddar and Creswell points',[10] so argues Conneller, and this view has been expressed before.[11] In many ways these penknife point assemblages are similar to the continental Federmesser industries.

The term 'Final Palaeolithic' was first introduced by Barton and Roberts[12] and it was this period that saw the temperature and conditions decline leading to a possibly complete abandonment of Britain. Jacobi,[13] however, noted an increase in Final Palaeolithic sites compared to preceding Creswellian sites and Conneller[14] argues that this could suggest a more permanent settlement pattern in a period of recolonisation. She further suggests it could, on the other hand, merely reflect different mobility and, settlement strategies and a shift towards more 'short-term' settlements in a variety,of different topographical locations, from more familiar settlements such as Creswell Crags. Perhaps this why only Mother Grundy's Parlour bears habitation evidence at Creswell in this period: because people were moving away from a more habitual environment. Incidentally, a Magdalenian retouched blade was found at Rookery Farm that was markedly similar to examples found at Mother Grundy's Parlour. Yet Rookery Farm has a much smaller assemblage than Mother Grundy's Parlour, suggesting a different kind of occupation, and is more comparable to Fox Hole Cave in the Peak District. At this point, let us consider Fox Hole Cave in more detail.

In his report on his excavations at Fox Hole Cave, Bramwell was unsure whether the occupation of the cave dated to the Mesolithic or the Late Upper Palaeolithic, but described a presence of horse which he believed attested to an open landscape with extensive grasslands. The discovery of three flints at the site - 'a shouldered point, core trimming flake and a truncated blade'[15] - hinted more towards a Late Upper Palaeolithic date than a Mesolithic one however. Things were slightly complicated, though, by the discovery of a penknife point in Layer D of the First Chamber which then seemed to attest to a Final Palaeolithic occupation. Also from Layer D, in the Bear Chamber, came a well-worked rod of deer antler: 'the implement bears a slightly hollow bevel at each end so would not appear to be of much use as a lance point.'[16] Nevertheless, it is of comparable style to other Late Upper Palaeolithic examples.

A fascinating find was the purposeful burial of a brown bear skull, which was placed on some rocks and then covered over by a flat slab. It proved difficult to discern which levels the burial related to so dating it proved difficult though Bramwell believed it 'agreed best with the Mesolithic / Upper Palaeolithic stratum'[17] Excavations in the Entrance Chamber discovered a 'fine brown bear skull and bones'[18] and within Fox Hole generally two types of bear were noted - potholers who initially explored what was

---

[9] Conneller InvesHgaHon of a Final Palaeolithic site at Rookery Farm, 2009
[10] Ibid. p. 179
[11] see Garrod The Upper Palaealithic Age in Britain (1926), Campbell The Upper Palaealithic of Britain (1977), Jacobi The Creswellian, Creswell and Cheddar (1991)
[12] Barton, R.N.E & Roberts, A Reviewing the British Late Upper Palaeolithic; new evidence for chronological patterning in the Lateglacial record, in Oxford Journal of Archaealogy, 15 (3), 1996, pp. 245-65
[13] Jacobi The Creswellian, Creswell and Cheddar (1991)
[14] Conneller Investigation of a Final Palaeolithic site at Rookery Farm, 2009
[15] Bramwell, D Excavations at Fox Hole Cave, High Wheeldon, Derbyshire, in Derbyshire Archaeological Journal, 91,1971, p. 11
[16] Ibid. p. 11
[17] Ibid. p. 11
[18] Ibid. p. 1

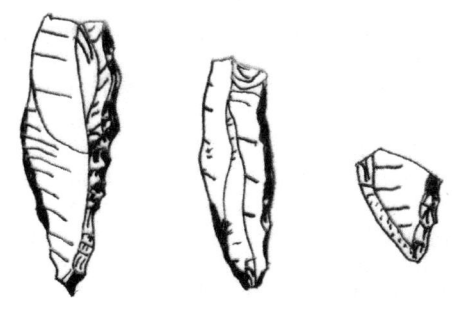

7.2 - Penknife points from the Final Palaeolithic site at Rookery Farm
(M. Beresford, redrawn from Conneller, 2009)

to become the Bear Chamber found several large bones of bear. In the Beaker layer a significant amount of brown bear remains were noted and many of these had been broken. Bramwell believed 'it is fairly clear that these early agriculturalists were regularly hunting the animals to rid them from their herding areas'[19] So it seems that bear was a significant presence throughout early prehistory and so the burial may have had some special significance due to this, although we cannot be sure when the skull was buried. Under Layer D further bear remains were noted proving its presence prior to the Final Palaeolithic occupation, so there is no reason why it could not date to this period, and ritualistic use of animal skulls are known in Late Upper Palaeolithic cave sites (such as at Chauvet, France, where a bear skull was placed on top of a rock similar to Fox Hole). It is interesting that it is again the skull that appears important, and this perhaps reflects spiritual beliefs with the head of the deceased, and this continues into the Neolithic -long barrows are predominated by skulls and long bones. Bramwell says that numerous specimens of brown bear were also noted in Layer E and these 'glacial' or Ice Age forms of the animal were around 20% larger than post-Ice Age examples and fitted into Kurten's study of Pleistocene Mammals.[20] There was also noted part of a lower jaw and some paw bones from Cave Lion, and both lion and bear were recovered from Robin Hood Cave, Creswell Crags. So there seems to be a special connection between the bears of the cave and the Palaeolithic people, and this seems to be Final Palaeolithic in date rather than Creswellian.

So it seems that many of the old haunts of the Late Upper Palaeolithic peoples had a continued life-span beyond this period and into the Final Palaeolithic / Mesolithic transition. Although much of the evidence of landscape use and settlement sites are lost under the North Sea, we can still gain a glimpse of what movement patterns and exploitation of resources occurred further to the west. If we compare and contrast Creswellian / Magdalenian sites across Europe with Final Palaeolithic / Federmesser sites we see the former being a lot larger with more emphasis on fauna such as horse or reindeer and the latter being much smaller. This could be evidence of smaller groups moving smaller distances but more frequently, as Conneller has suggested.[21] Equally it may be that they did not have carry tools or resources with them but relied instead on known deposits of local raw material- in essence 'foragers not collectors.'[22] However, if they were abandoning familiar, known sites for new settlement areas, it begs the question as to how they could be certain of obtaining this raw material. More likely it was another adaptation to changing hunting environments.

The warmer climate and shifting flora with pioneering species such as birch taking hold would have seen large-size herd animals such as horse and reindeer make way for animals like red and roe deer - remember the red deer stag art at Church Hole

---

[19] Ibid. p. 8
[20] Kurten, B Pleistocene Mammals of Europe, 1968
[21] Conneller Investigation of a Final Palaeolithic site at Rookery Farm, 2009, p. 181
[22] Ibid. p. 181

cave though, suggesting an importance for this animal as early as 12,700 years ago. Over the wider landscape 'Creswellian sites have been understood as elements in a logistical settlement system, with residential sites (possibly Farndon Fields), field camps (Gough's Cave, Robin Hood Cave) and task sites (upland sites such as Fox Hole Cave). These contrast with the use of predominantly local raw material sources in the Final Palaeolithic and, in general, the small size of the sites ... Rookery Farm fits this pattern.'[23] Whilst I would agree with this, we have to remember flint was not a local resource to any of these Creswellian sites, so open sites closer to flint sources could well have existed on a similar small scale in this period also. Recent research[24] has suggested that majoritively the Creswell flint was procured in the south-west of Britain, whilst at Seamer K, North Yorkshire much of the lithic material was made from local Wolds flint.[25] Some of the tools from Seamer K, however, were made from material sourced from glacial tills in all probability from the plains of Doggerland, and here again we have a connection to the resource-rich landscape of Doggerland and settlement areas further to the west in Britain. It could be, though, that the inhabitants were actually from Doggerland itself and travelled to Seamer K to exploit the natural resources there (rather than vice-versa) as the site is located on the edge of a lake which would have provided valuable resources on top of the local flint.

Finally, let us look at the Final Palaeolithic sites to the north of Creswell and try and understand how the landscape was being used as we moved into the Mesolithic period after the ice had gone. Fieldwork at Misterton Carr revealed the largest collection of lithic material in the whole of north Nottinghamshire suggesting much was going on here. The site lies approximately 5-6 miles due west of the Trent which again may suggest people from Doggerland were using the river systems to find their way there. Furthermore a series of smaller tributaries, such as the rivers Idle, Turne, Don and Went, flow into the Trent in this region providing an easy to follow 'route map' for the area. Site 1 at Misterton Carr had by far the largest concentration of flints, with 2,025 of the 3,808 flints found at the entire site recovered here. These flints, however, spanned the Mesolithic, Neolithic and Early Bronze Age (a several thousand year time-span) making it difficult to understand what had been going on.[26] What is apparent, though, is that a local raw material source was utilised, and this also reflects the resource choice at Rookery Farm that we saw earlier. Radley[27] has also noted this to have occurred at the earlier Creswellian site at Brigham in Yorkshire, and other 'broad blade' sites across the area, so we could be seeing a pattern emerging over a large area.

Other similarities exist at Misterton Carr in relation to other sites. Around three quarters of the flint tools recovered there are of Mesolithic date, although some of them may well be Final Palaeolithic: 'the presence of tranchet axes and the predominance of simple obliquely blunted points clearly relates the Misterton Carr sites to the Maglemosian tradition, with many similarities to the English type-site of Star Carr in the North Riding of Yorkshire.'[28] Buckland and Dolby have also pointed out sites with flint tools that, although at first believed to be Late Upper Palaeolithic, may well be of Final Palaeolithic date instead - an end scraper was recovered at the site of Messingham near Scunthorpe and a peat sample dated the context it was found in to c.10,280 ± 120 BP.

---

[23] Conneller Investigotion of a Final Palaeolithic site at Rookery Farm, 2009, p. 182
[24] Rockman, M Landscape Learning in the Late Glacial Recolonisation of Britain, 2003, Unpublished PhD thesis, University of Arizona
[25] Conneller Investigation of a Final Palaeolithic site at Rookery Farm, 2009, p. 183
[26] Buckland, P.C. & Dolby, M.J. Mesolithic and later material from Mistertan Carr, Nottinghamshire, in Transactions of the Thoroton Society, 77, 1973, p. 6
[27] Radley, J A Mesolithic structure at Sheldon with a note on chert as a raw material on Mesolithic sites in the South Pennines, in Derbyshire Archaeological Journal, 88, 1968, pp. 26-36
[28] Buckland & Dolby Mesolithic and later material from Misterton Carr, 1973, p. 23

And again, at Brigham, a collection of flints were discovered that were made of the same poor, grey-white flint as that at Misterton, so again could be of a similar date. Manby,[29] however, believed the site to be Creswellian in date based on the backed pieces found there . Not to be dissuaded, Buckland and Dolby believe the collection of flint tools from Brigham actually shares many similarities to those found at Misterton Carr, which suggests a later Final Palaeolithic / Mesolithic date rather than a Creswellian.[30] Clearly, a close study of known sites and flint collections is needed in order to create a much more accurate picture of the transitional period right at the very end of the Ice Age. However, through these few examples alone we can see the story beginning to unfold.

The geology of the area can also shed light onto what was happening right at the end of the last Ice Age as it seems 'deposits were disturbed by frost action during Zone III which puts Sheffield's Hill, Brigham and Misterton Carr in a post-Late Glacial period similar to Star Carr.'[31] This seems to confirm the archaeology just discussed and places the sites at the beginning of the Mesolithic, although we must remember that no transition happens overnight. The site of Star Carr has been discussed previously but again new evidence and theories have emerged relatively recently, and opinion has certainly changed since it was first discovered. Clark's initial belief was that red and roe deer were exploited and that the site was occupied during the winter to process the antlers of these into the (suggested) head dresses discussed in chapter 4. The Mesolithic people would then follow the deer over the uplands in the summer before returning in the winter.[32] Mike Pitts, however, has recently argued that the site was a 'factory' from which bone points were made from the antlers, as opposed to a temporary settlement or camp.[33] As antler needs to be softened before it can be worked, this may be why a large number of antlers were observed at the site which were awaiting 'processing'. As Pitts further argued, just because the antler was shed in the winter does not mean that is when the site was used - it could have been transported to the site at any time of the year and stored in a cache. What we do know is that Star Carr, whatever its purpose, is one of the earliest Mesolithic sites in Britain and probably fits into the much wider distribution of sites currently being discussed, not discounting the multitude of sites within Doggerland that are now lost to us. In other words, we are probably only seeing a fraction of the overall picture in the Final Palaeolithic and into the Mesolithic.

Further sites of this date in the general area are known at Pike Low, Mickleden and Deepcar to the west of Sheffield, at Hatfield to the east of Doncaster, at Cove Farm, Haxey, at Eastfield Farm, Tickhill and at Westfield Farm, Tuxford. These select examples show an abundance of post-Creswellian sites in the area to the north of Creswell Crags. The severe climate at the end of the Ice Age may have driven people away from the area, but they soon returned once the climate improved it would seem. Such an abundance in a relatively small area in some ways supports the theory that Final Palaeolithic and Mesolithic peoples inhabited more sites but perhaps in smaller groups, although the sites within the Creswell Heritage Area and in the Peak District were more suited to small hunting parties so may well skew the more general trends for wider Britain in the period. From the later Neolithic and onwards evidence seems to suggest that rather than being abandoned many of the Late Upper Palaeolithic sites were continually used throughout prehistory. Indeed, many reflect use in the Late Upper Palaeolithic, Mesolithic, Neolithic and Bronze Age, and more work needs to be done on this before conclusive answers are reached.

---

[29] Manby, TG. A Creswellian site at Brigham, East Yorkshire, in Anthropological Journal, 1966, p. 211
[30] Buckland & Dolby Mesolithic and later material from Misterton Carr, 1973, p. 35
[31] Ibid. p. 25
[32] see Clark, J.G.D. Excavations at Star Carr, 1954 and Clark J.G.D. Star Carr: a case study in Bioarchaeology, 1972

[33] Pitts, M Hides and antlers: a new look at the gatherer-hunter site of Star Carr, North Yorkshire, England, 1979

7.3 - The Abbots Bromley Horn Dancers, circa. 1915, wearing antler headdresses similar to those found at Star Carr. Were they for ritual, hunting or a ceremonial dance?
(Public Domain)

7.4 - Prehistoric toolmaker John Lord making replica Ice Age tools during an event at Creswell Crags
(© Creswell Heritage Trust)

8

Conclusion

Throughout this book we have seen the changes that have occurred at Creswell Crags over the course of its history. The climate and the landscape have altered dramatically, with hot temperatures and hippos wallowing in its river around 120,000 years ago, to extreme colds and open, tundra landscapes and woolly mammoths roaming the gorge around 50,000 years ago. Then the ice disappeared for a final time around 10,000 years ago, taking with it the arctic fauna and leaving behind red and roe deer with the land quickly becoming wooded. Neanderthals have come and gone to be replaced by our ancestors, the modern humans, although this was perhaps not as foregone as we might think:

> *'there was nothing inevitable about the triumph of the Moderns, and a twist of Pleistocene fate could have left the Neanderthals occupying Europe to this day. The 30,000 years by which we have missed them represent only a few ticks of the Ice Age clock'.*[1]

Those Neanderthals first came to Creswell Crags some 60,000 years ago and utilised its caves and the surrounding landscape for at least 15,000 years. What happened to the Neanderthals at Creswell when Modern Man turned up somewhere around 45,000 years ago may well never be known, but something did happen and, whatever that something was, when the dust settled only Modern Man was left. Unlike the typical 'cave man' image, that Modern Man wore clothes including gloves and shoes, wore body jewellery such as pendants and bracelets, and created art on the walls of their cave. They hunted arctic hare and deer and used the carcasses to make bone tools, weapons and even sewing kits. But more importantly, they traveled around a vast Ice Age world, obtaining resources from as far apart as flint from southern Britain and amber from the Baltic, and all these tools, weapons, possessions and art were left behind to help us understand who are ancestors were and how they lived over ten thousand years ago.

---

[1] Stringer, C & Gamble, C In Search af the Neanderthals, 1993, p. 219

As we have seen, much of our current knowledge has emerged through years of meticulous work, and this knowledge continues to grow. It appears one of the last, possibly the last, Neanderthal site has been found in a cave in Gibraltar, dating to a good five thousand years or so later than the supposed extinction date of 35,000 years ago. And in the last year or so, two further sites have revealed what seems to be Late Upper Palaeolithic art, a mammoth engraving at Cheddar and a reindeer on the Gower Peninsula, although it is still early days for these discoveries. There can be no doubt, given all that has been discussed in this book, that the days of the 'Creswellian' are numbered, and that the early inhabitants of what is now Britain were not isolated but rather part of an entire Ice Age landscape. They traveled from Germany, Holland and Belgium, across an entire landscape that is now buried deep under the sea, and utilised as much of the British landscape's resources as they could. And at the heart of that British landscape lies Creswell Crags, currently the base for the Limestone Journeys project, a project which helps to celebrate, conserve and manage the hugely important landscape of the Magnesian Limestone ridge. That same ridge that our Ice Age ancestors stood on for 50,000 years and watched herds of mammoth and reindeer wander slowly into the distance.

Today, that scene has long gone, but the story has not. The site of Creswell Crags now boasts a new, state of the art visitor center to showcase that story and, perhaps more significantly, it also receives worldwide recognition as a hugely important archaeological site. It may seem ironic that the people who visit the site and learn about our Ice Age past do so in a period that sits in one of the most stable climates in the past 500,000 years. Indeed, since the end of the last Ice Age the population has grown from just a few million to around six billion in the present. Human occupation of Britain (approximately the last 850,000 years) has seen a number of changes and cycles that 'have pushed Earth to ever-greater swings of climate, with the added superimposition of short-term fluctuations lasting a few millennia. The last of these really severe global climatic blips was the Younger Dryas of about 13,000 years ago.'[2] As we have seen, this drove our 'Creswell Man' out of Britain, and when he returned as 'Mesolithic Man' he bore witness to the start of the Holocene, the present interglacial that we inhabit today.

Chris Stringer and his team in the Ancient Human Occupation of Britain project ask the question that, given Earth's extreme climatic fluctuations in the past, are we witnessing climate change in the present as part of this natural cycle? It is difficult to say and although we are undoubtedly adding to the process with our actions it could be that we are simply in 'unknown territory'. Going on past cycles, Earth should have been seeing the start of another cooling phase, with a major glaciation in around 50,000 years time. Some scientists argue that rising greenhouse gases are in fact affecting this process and preventing the cooling that we should now be seeing. The scientific community almost resign to the idea that this global warming will see a 3°C rise in temperature, which could put up to a billion people in danger of starvation due to lost arable lands and water shortages.[3]

Let us look at the facts:
- Northern oceans have seen a 7% increase in freshwater runoffs flowing into them in the last eighty years. This is from melting ice and accelerated drainage.
- The Arctic now has a seasonal 'ice-free' state for the first time in a million years
- The Antarctic has changed radically: sea ice has reduced by 20% in the last sixty years and the Ross Sea is freshening through an increase in melting ice sheets

---

[2] Stringer, C Hama Britannicus, 2006, p. 162
[3] Ibid, p. 163

- If the most vulnerable ice sheets - those of Greenland and west Antarctica start to melt with the inevitable 3°C rise, then many coastal cities (including London, New York, Hong Kong and Tokyo) would be lost through flooding
- For Britain, just a one metre rise in sea levels would affect London, Hull, Liverpool, the south coast and much of East Anglia

So it seems we are destined to see a warming of temperatures, but the in-flow of freezing glacial melt-waters could instead see a rapid cooling in the seas and oceans, leading to a dramatic drop in temperature in certain areas, particularly the North Atlantic. In the past, the North Atlantic conveyor has 'shut down' or reversed, so instead of bringing warming currents to the area they have been transported away, leading to extreme drops in temperature in western Europe. A drop of around 10°C in the Atlantic would mean a reduction in temperature of around 4°C in western Europe.

Let us hope, then, that we can learn from our past in order to safeguard our future. As Stringer and Gamble quite nicely put it: 'we should celebrate our rich and varied prehistory as a route to enhancing, in these multi-cultural times, our understanding of ourselves'.[4] Thirty-five thousand years ago we survived and the Neanderthals became extinct. If another Ice Age arrives, next time we might not be so lucky.

---

[4] Stringer, C & Gamble, C In Search of the Neanderthals, 1993, p. 219

Appendix: Instruments for Cave-Hunting

by William Boyd Dawkins
taken from *Cave-hunting* (1874)

The instruments which Mr. James Parker, Mr. Ayshford Sanford and myself have found most valuable in cave-hunting, apart from the tools of the workman, are as follows:

1. A hammer with an ash handle about twenty inches long, inserted into a square head of best steel, ending in a chisel edge in the same plane as the handle, weighing almost eight ounces, and seven inches in length.
2. A steel chisel ten inches long.
3. A prismatic compass.
4. A thermometer for taking the temperatures of the air and water.
5. An aneroid.
6. A steel measuring tape.
7. Abney's patent level which is used for laying down datum-line for plan, as well as for taking the dips and angles.
8. A stout rope not less than twenty feet long with a horse's girth at the end is necessary for the exploration of vertical fissures, so that the explorer may be let down without any great danger.
9. In the exploration of water-caves, in which there are sheets of water of considerable size and depth, a raft may be used, such as that devised by Mr. James Parker for the navigation of the great cave of Wookey Hole.
10. The most convenient lights for use in caves are the common composite candles. Paraffin candles are open to the objection that they gutter, lanthorns do not give a sufficiently diffused light, and the smoke of paraffin torches, or flambeaux dipped in turpentine or tar is intolerable.

Bibliography

Primary Sources

TNA – Creswell letters
DRO – publicity leaflets
CCRL – ALA 5/1, Armstrong Collection, letter between Don Brothwell and Dr. Owen of University Museum, Manchester dated 14th February 1962
NRO – Nottinghamshire County Council Minutes (printed), Finance Committee 30th January 1912

Printed Primary Sources

The Pall Mall Gazette, Friday April 20th, 1876, Issue 3796
The Derby Mercury, Wednesday 9th October, 1878, Issue 854
Daily News, Monday 25th August, 1879, Issue 10405
The Derby Mercury, Wednesday 27th August, 1879, Issue 8591
The Times, Palaeolithic Man in England: New Light on Age of the Cavemen, 22nd December, 1924
British Archaeology, September 2003, pp. 9-13
Before Farming, 2003/3 (10)
The Guardian, Thursday 15th April, 2004
Antiquity, Vol. 78, No. 300, June 2004
Creswell Crags Museum & Archaeology Park: A Potted History of Creswell Crags and the Heritage Trust, Business Plan – Appendix 4, 2003
Current Archaeology, No. 197, May/June 2005
Archaeology and Conservation in Derbyshire, Issue 6, January 2009
Worksop Guardian, 8th May, 2009

Electronic (as of September 2009)

Capra 5, 2003, available online at: http://capra.group.shef.ac.uk/5/pettitt.pdf
English Heritage Research Agenda: Creswell Crags ice age rock art, available online at: http://www.helm.org.uk/upload/pdf/Research_Agenda2005.pdf
Learning from curves: the female figure in Palaeolithic Europe, Pamela Russell, May 2006, Rock Art Research, available online at: http://findarticles.com/p/articles/mi_6922/is_1_23/ai_n28429503/
Virtually the Ice Age: http://www.creswell-crags.org.uk/virtuallytheiceage/index.html
The British Mountaineering Council website: http://www.thebmc.co.uk/Feature.aspx?id=1843

Secondary Sources

Armstrong, A L *3rd Interim Report of the Committee for the exploration of Caves in the Derbyshire district, Report of the British Association for the Advancement of Science,* July 1924
Armstrong, A L *Excavations at Mother Grundy's Parlour,* 1924, *Journal of the Royal Anthropological Institute,* Vol. LV
Armstrong, A L *The Pin Hole Cave,* 1926, report to the British Association for the Advancement of Science, (Unpublished)
Armstrong, A L (1924-6) Press cuttings relating to 1924-26 excavations at Creswell Crags, Source unknown. Creswell Crags Visitor Centre Archive
Armstrong, A L & Garrod, D A E *5th Interim Report of the Committee for the exploration of Caves in the Derbyshire district, Report of the British Association for the Advancement of Science, Section H, Anthropology,* 1927
Armstrong, A L *Excavations at Creswell Crags, Pin Hole Cave, 1925-28,* 1929, *Transactions of The Hunter Archaeological Society,* Vol. III
Armstrong, A L *Discovery of an Engraved Drawing of a Masked Human Figure,* 1929, in *Proceedings of the Prehistoric Society,* Vol. VI
Armstrong, A L *Excavations at Creswell Crags, Derbyshire 1928-32: The Pin Hole Cave,* 1937, *Transactions of The Hunter Archaeological Society,* Vol. IV
Armstrong, A L *A Bull-roarer of Le Moustier age from Pin Hole Cave, Creswell Crags, Derbyshire,* 1939, *Antiquaries Journal,* 16
Armstrong *28th Interim report of the Committee for the exploration of Caves in the Derbyshire district,* Report to the British Association, Section H, Anthropology, (unpublished), 1956,
Armstrong *29th Interim report of the Committee for the exploration of Caves in the Derbyshire district,* Report to the British Association, Section H, Anthropology, (unpublished), 1957
Bahn, P et al *Written in Bones,* (Newton Abbot), 2002
Bahn, P & Pettitt, P *Britain's Oldest Art,* (Swindon), 2009, pp. 16-35
Barton, N, Roberts, A J and Roe, D A (eds), *The Late Glacial in north-west Europe: human adaptation and environmental change at the end of the Pleistocene,* CBA Research Report No. 77, 1991
Bateman, T *Vestiges of the Antiquities of Derbyshire,* (Cromford), 2009

Bohmers, A *Statistics and graphs in the study of flint assemblages: II A preliminary report on the statistical analysis of the Younger Palaeolithic in northwestern Europe,* 1956, *Palaeohistoria,* 5, pp.7-25

Boyd Dawkins, W *Cave-hunting,* (London), 1874

Boyd Dawkins, W *On the mammal fauna of Creswell Caves,* 1877, *Quaternary Journal of the Geological Society,* Vol.33

Boyd Dawkins, W *On the Evidence Afforded by the Caves of Great Britain as to the Antiquity of Man,* 1878, *The Journal of the Anthropological Institute of Great Britain and Ireland,* Vol. 7

Boyd Dawkins, W & Mello, J M *Further discoveries in the Creswell Caves,* 1879, *Quaternary Journal of the Geological Society,* Vol. XXXV

Bramwell, D et al *Ossom's Cave, Staffordshire: A study of its Vertebrate remains and Late Pleistocene Environments,* in *Staffordshire Archaeological Studies,* 4, 1987

Brothwell, D R *Digging up Bones,* (New York), 1981

Brown, C *A History of Nottinghamshire* (Unknown), 1896

Campbell, J B *The Upper Palaeolithic of Britain,* (Oxford), 1977, (2 Volumes)

Charles, R & Jacobi, R *The Late Glacial fauna from the Robin Hood Cave, Creswell Crags: a re-assessment,* in *Oxford Journal of Archaeology,* 13, 1994

Clark, J G D *Excavations at Star Carr,* (Cambridge) 1954

Colcutt, S N *The Stratigraphy of Creswell Crags,* 1975, Unpublished dissertation for the degree of M.A.(Hons) at Edinburgh University

Coolidge, F L & Wynn, T *The Rise of Homo Sapiens: the Evolution of Modern Thinking,* (Chichester), 2009

Cooper, L & Jacobi, R *Two Late Glacial finds from north-west Leicestershire* in *Transactions of the Leicestershire Archaeological and Historical Society,* 75 (2001)

Cooper, L *A Creswellian campsite, Newtown Linford* in *Transactions of the Leicestershire Archaeological and Historical Society,* 76 (2002),

Cunliffe, B *The Oxford Illustrated History of Prehistoric Europe,* (Oxford), 2001

Darvill, T *Prehistoric Britain,* (London), 1998

Davies, G, Badcock, A, Mills, N & Smith, B *The Creswell Crags Limestone Heritage Area Management Action Plan,* (unpublished), 2004

Duarte, C, Mauricio, J, Pettitt, P B, Souto, P, Trinkhaus, E, van der Plicht, H and Zilhao, J *The early Upper Palaeolithic human skeleton from the Abrigo do Lagar Velho (Portugal) and modern human emergence in Iberia,* Proceedings of the National Academy of Sciences, June 22, 1999, vol. 96, no. 13

Dundes, A *A Psychoanalytic study of the Bullroarer, Man,* New Series, Vol. 11, No. 2 (Jun., 1976), pp. 220-238 (Royal Anthropological Institute of Great Britain and Ireland)

Gamble, C *The Palaeolithic Settlement of Europe,* (Cambridge), 1986

Gamble, C *Grave shortcomings; the evidence for Neanderthal burial,* in *Current Anthropology,* 30, 1989

Garrod, D *The Upper Palaeolithic Age in Britain,* (Oxford), 1926

Hall, M A & Pettitt, P B *A pair of merels boards on a stone block from Church Hole cave, Creswell Crags, Nottinghamshire, England,* (unpublished), 2008

Halverson, J *Art for art's sake in the Palaeolithic,* in *Current Anthropology,* vol. 28, 1987

Hart, C R *The North Derbyshire Archaeological Survey,* (Sheffield), 1984

Heath, T *Pleistocene Deposits of Derbyshire,* 1882, *Derbyshire Archaeological Journal,* Vol. IV

Huyghe, R *Larousse encyclopedia of Prehistoric & Ancient Art,* (London), 1957

Jackson, J.W. *The Creswell Caves, Journal of the British Scientific Association,* Vol. VI, No. 41, 1967

Jenkinson, R D S *Creswell Crags: Late Pleistocene Sites in the East Midlands,* BAR British Series 122, (Oxford) 1984

Kitching, J W *Bone, tooth and Horn Tools of Palaeolithic Man: an Account of the Osteodontokeratic Discoveries in the Pin Hole Cave, Derbyshire,* (Manchester), 1963

Kuhn, S. L. *"Unpacking" reduction: lithic raw material economy in the Mousterian of West-Central Italy, Journal of Anthropological Archaeology,* 10, 1991

Laing, R *On the bone caves of Creswell and the discovery of an extinct Pliocene Feline (Felis brevirostris) new to Great Britain, Reports to the British Association for the Advancement of Science,* (Newcastle), 1889

Leakey, R *The Making of Mankind,* (New York), 1981

Legg, A J & Rowley-Conwy, P A *Star Carr Revisited,* (London) 1988

Lewin, R *Human Evolution: an illustrated introduction,* 3rd edition, (Cambridge, MA), 1993

Lewis-Williams, D *The Mind in the Cave: consciousness and the origins of art,* (London), 2008

Martindale, C *Cognition and Consciousness,* (Homewood, Illinois), 1981

Mellars, P & Stringer, C (eds) *The Human Revolution: Behavioural and Biological Perspectives on the Origins of Modern Humans,* (Edinburgh), 1989

Mello, J M *On some bone-caves in Creswell Crags,* 1875, *Quaternary Journal of the Geological Society,* Vol. 31

Mello, J M *Palaeolithic Man at Creswell,* 1879, *Derbyshire Archaeological Journal,* Vol. I

Mello, J M & Heath, T *On the exploration of Creswell caves,* 1880, *Transactions of the Manchester Geological Society,* Vol. XIV, part IV

Metz, WH, van Beek, BL, Steegstra, H (eds.) *Patina: Essays presented to Jay Jordan Butler on the Occasion of his 80th birthday,* (Amsterdam / Groningen), 2001

Mithen, S *The Prehistory of the mind,* (London), 1998

Mithen, S *After the Ice: A Global Human History, 20,000-5000BC,* (London), 2003

Mullins, E.H. *Langwith Cave, Transactions of the East Derbyshire Field Club,* 1907, pp. 32-34

Mullins, E.H. *The Ossiferous Cave at Langwith, The Derbyshire Archaeological and Natural History Journal,* Vol. 35, 1913, pp. 137-158

Oakley, K P *Relative dating of the fossil hominids of Europe, Bulletin of the Natural History Museum Geology Series,* Vol. XLI, (34 (1)), (London), 1980, pp. 1-63

Pettitt, P, Bahn, P & Ripoll, S *Palaeolithic cave art at Creswell Crags in wider European context,* (Oxford) 2007

Pike, A W G et al *Verification of the age of the Palaeolithic cave art at Creswell Crags, UK, Journal of Archaeological Science* 32 (2005) pp.1649-1655

Pryor, F *Britain BC,* (London), 2003

Renfrew, C *British Prehistory,* (London), 1974

Ruddy, M *Water vole (Arvicola) tooth morphology: exploring shape to examine evolution,* abstract from a paper given at the First Workshop of AHOB2, London, 10-11th October, 2007

Sollas, W G *Ancient Hunters and their Modern Representatives,* (London) 1924

Stiner, M C *The faunal remains at Grotta Guattari: a taphonomic perspective, Current Anthropology,* 32 (2), 1991

Stringer, C and Gamble, C *In Search of the Neanderthals,* (New York), 1993
Stringer, C *Homo Britannicus,* (London), 2006
Wymer, J *The Palaeolithic Age,* (Beckenham), 1984

Index

A

Ancient Hunters (Sollas) 14, 26
Arctic hare 45, 47, 57, 58, 63, 88, 101
Arcy-sur-Cure 45
Armstrong, Alan Leslie 2, 22-35, 54, 59-60, 62, 64-66, 72-75, 77, 89-91
Ash Tree Cave 76, 89-91
Association for the Advancement of Science 22, 74, 91
Aurignacian 23, 26-32, 45, 52, 91
Awls 17, 23, 25, 30, 57-59, 90,
Axes 23, 24, 99

B

Bahn, Paul 26, 36-37, 39-42, 49, 52, 55, 58, 85, 87-88
Bear 6, 8, 10, 15, 19, 20, 23, 30, 34, 59, 74, 96-97
Bird (engraving) 38
Bird / female (panel) 38, 40-41, 43, 45-47
Bison 5-6, 15, 19-21, 24, 28, 32, 85
Bison-engraving 25-26, 38, 49
Boat House Cave 34
Bone tools 25, 27, 32, 50, 83, 93, 101
Bones (see human remains)
Bronze Age 3, 64, 68, 76, 85, 98, 100
Buckland, William 3-6

C

Campbell, John 8, 52, 57, 58, 59, 71-76, 96
Cave art 2, 3, 14, 26, 30, 35, 36-49, 63, 69, 70, 71, 93
Châtelperronian 23, 27, 81-83
Chauvet 37, 97
Cheddar Gorge 45, 50, 52, 53, 58, 69, 71, 84, 88, 89, 102
Cheddar point 52, 53, 56, 77, 91, 95-96
Church Hole 3, 5, 9, 10, 12, 17-21, 26, 28-30, 36-49, 54, 58-60, 62, 64, 67, 70, 76-77, 86, 98
Cook, Jill 88
Creswell Crags
Creswell Heritage Area 56, 64, 76, 88, 90, 100,
    Museum & Education Centre 68-69
Creswell point 52,53, 57, 60, 91, 96
Creswellian 2, 3, 29, 35, 37, 42, 45-47, 49, 50-62, 83, 90, 91, 96, 97, 98, 99, 100, 102,

D

Dating
    animal bones 73, 97
    archaeology 23, 32, 52, 58, 68, 76, 85, 102
        cave art 37, 45

human remains 62, 64, 76, 89, 91
Dawkins, William Boyd 5, 11, 12, 14-21, 22, 24, 26, 29, 30, 58, 59, 64, 65, 74, 75, 85, 88, 89
Doggerland 18, 47-48, 50, 93-95, 98, 100
Dordogne 47, 50

E

Engravings 26, 36-49, 85

F

Farndon Fields 55, 98
Final Palaeolithic 53, 95, 96, 97, 98, 99, 100
Flint
  knapping 55, 95
tools 11, 12, 15, 19, 20, 21, 25, 32, 50, 53, 54-56, 60, 71, 80, 83, 91, 93, 94, 98-99, 101
  resource 27, 80-81, 98, 101
Font Robert point 23, 45
Fox Hole cave 60, 96-98
Funerary practice 48, 54, 62, 69, 71-77, 82, 83, 84, 90-91, 95, 97

G

Garrod, Dorothy 3, 8, 26, 28-30, 47, 52, 53, 54, 60, 62, 91,
Gough's Cave 45, 58, 59, 62, 69, 71-74, 89, 98
Graffiti 37, 39, 42, 65
Gravettian 27, 45

H

Head-cult 71, 76, 84, 97
Hearths 23, 27, 80, 83
Heath, Thomas 11-12, 16-17, 59
Hippo 6, 18, 20, 21, 63, 101
Horse
  Art 12, 14, 16, 21, 26, 29, 38, 41, 49, 54, 62, 69, 85, 88
    Hunting 87, 88

Human remains 34, 35, 62, 64, 71-77, 84, 89, 90, 92
Hunting practices 8, 23, 28, 50, 53-54, 57, 60, 81, 82, 84-88, 91, 97, 98, 100
Hyaena 4, 5, 10, 11, 12, 17, 18, 20, 21, 24, 25, 28, 86, 91

I

Ice Age 1, 2, 3, 8, 36, 37, 38, 39, 40, 50, 52, 55, 57, 59, 60, 61, 62, 63, 69, 78, 80, 85, 89, 92, 97, 100, 101, 102
Iron Age 24, 64, 76, 91

J

Jackson, Wilfrid 29
Jacobi, Roger 3, 26, 46, 52, 54, 55, 57, 58, 59, 60, 68, 96
Jenkinson, Rogan 34, 35, 67, 72, 74, 75, 76

K

Kent's Cavern 11, 28
Kesslerloch 12, 18
Kirkdale Cave 3, 5
Knives 83, 95, 96, 97

L

La Madeleine 28
Laing, Robert 74, 75
Langwith Cave 91
Last Glacial Maximum 62
Last Interglacial 102
Late Upper Palaeolithic 3, 8, 37, 39, 45, 46, 49, 50, 52, 53, 54, 55, 57, 58, 60, 64, 69, 71, 74, 86, 90, 95, 96, 97, 99, 100, 102
Leaf point 45, 58, 74
Lithics 83, 96
Lynx 72

M

Magdalenian 3, 22, 23, 28-32, 35, 36, 40, 41, 42, 45, 46, 48, 49, 52, 54, 60, 62, 63, 77, 83, 90, 96, 97
Magnesian Limestone 1, 6, 50, 102
Mammoth 6, 9, 10, 14, 15, 19, 20, 21, 22, 23, 24, 25, 27, 28, 29, 32, 53, 54, 57, 63, 85, 101, 102
Manchester Museum 29, 34,
Markland Grips 76
Mello, Rev. John Magens 3, 5, 6, 8-12, 16, 21, 22, 26, 29, 58, 59, 62, 65, 74, 75
Mesolithic 27, 28, 31, 55, 57, 64, 68, 74, 90, 91, 95-100, 102
Modern humans (homo sapiens) 3, 24, 32, 55, 59, 60, 78-92, 101
Mother Grundy's Parlour 5, 18, 20, 21, 22-29, 34, 37, 38, 48, 55, 64, 68, 74, 75, 96
Mousterian 11, 23, 25, 30, 32, 83, 90, 91
Mullins, Rev. E.H. 14, 64, 90-91

N

Neanderthals 12, 21, 23, 24, 59, 60, 63, 78-92, 95, 101, 103
Needles 57, 59
Neolithic 3, 22, 29, 31, 55, 58, 60, 64, 66, 68, 74, 76, 85, 89, 91, 97, 98, 100
Niaux 48

O

Ochre 40, 85
Ossom's Cave 56

P

Paintings (cave) 39, 41, 49, 85
Palaeolithic 39, 40, 42, 45, 46, 48, 50, 52, 53, 54, 57, 58, 59, 60, 63, 64, 68, 71, 72, 74, 83, 85, 86, 90, 91, 92, 93, 96, 97, 98, 99, 100, 102
Parietal art 36, 48
Paviland Cave 3

Peak District 8, 47, 48, 50, 56, 60, 66, 67, 96, 100
Penknife point 95-97
Perigord 12
Pettitt, Paul 26, 37, 38, 40, 41, 45, 46, 49, 76, 77,
Pin Hole 5, 10-12, 22-25, 28, 28, 31, 32, 34, 37, 44, 45, 48, 49, 54, 58, 59, 66, 72, 75
Pin Hole Man 30-31, 49, 54, 59
Pyrenees 18

Q

Quartzite (tools) 10, 11, 12, 17, 21, 23, 24, 25, 30, 32, 58,

R

Radiocarbon dating 44, 45, 52, 57, 58, 62, 73, 76, 89, 91
Reindeer 8, 10, 15, 17, 18, 19, 20, 21, 22, 23, 25, 26, 27, 28, 29, 30, 34, 47, 50, 54, 57, 63, 88, 90, 91, 97, 98, 102,
Rhinoceros 6, 8, 9, 10, 15, 19, 31,
Ripoll, Sergio 37
Ritual 35, 57, 72, 76, 83, 84, 97, 100
Robin Hood Cave 5, 9-17, 20, 21, 26, 29, 30, 37, 38, 43, 45, 48, 49, 52, 55, 58, 59, 72, 73, 74, 75, 85, 87, 88, 97, 98
Roman 24, 64, 69, 76

S

Scrapers 23, 52, 55, 57, 74, 90, 91, 99
Sheffield University 34
Sollas, W J 14, 15, 26, 36
Solutrean 11, 21, 23, 27, 28, 29, 32, 54, 88
Stag engraving 38, 39, 40, 57, 98
Star Carr 57, 59, 62, 99
Stubbs, George 1-2

T
Thread winder 59

U
Uranium (U-Series) dating 43, 45

V
Venus figurine 46-47
Victorian excavations 9-21
Vulva engravings 37, 38, 40, 43

W
Welbeck Estate 66-67
Whaley rock shelter 55, 57, 76, 90
Wolf 6, 10, 15, 19, 20, 34, 59

Y
Yorkshire 3, 27, 34, 57, 59, 98, 99